Cian

2022.

Democracy, direct action and socialism

A debate on fundamentals

Michael Foot
Sean Matgamna

Second edition

Democracy, direct action and socialism

A debate on fundamentals

Michael Foot and Sean Matgamna

Printed by Imprint Digital, Exeter EX5 5HY
ISBN: 978-1-909639-24-9

Front cover: police arrest striker during 1984-5 miners' strike
Second edition. Published 2016 by Workers' Liberty

20E Tower Workshops
Riley Road
London SE1 3DG
020 7394 8923
awl@workersliberty.org
www.workersliberty.org

This work is licensed under the Creative Commons Attribution 2.5 Generic License.
To view a copy of this license, visit:
http://creativecommons.org/licenses/by/2.5/
or send a letter to Creative Commons, 444 Castro Street, Suite 900, Mountain View, California, 94041, USA.

Contents

Introduction *Martin Thomas* **3**

Introduction to the web edition **6**

Preface: Thatcherism and democracy *Sean Matgamna* **7**

The debate:

My kind of democracy *Michael Foot* **22**

Democracy, direct action and socialism *Sean Matgamna* **43**
    Margaret Thatcher and democracy **43**
    Is direct action against an elected
    capitalist government undemocratic? **46**
    The scarecrow of Stalinism **60**
    Superstition or the class struggle? **69**

The Conway Hall debate:

Democracy and direct action *Martin Thomas* **84**

What revolutionary socialists advocated against Thatcher *Sean Matgamna* **89**
    The class struggle left in 1980 **89**
    Stop the Thatcher blitz! **92**
    We need a workers' government! **97**

Baksheesh:

Trotsky's Diary in Exile *Michael Foot* **103**

Michael Foot: the man who embraced defeat to avoid defeat *Sean Matgamna* **105**

Can socialism make sense?

A book which makes the case for socialism.

At a time when more and more people call themselves socialists, and a self-confessed socialist is leader of the Labour Party, this book explores what socialism means, whether it can rise again, how and why.

Answering questions such as: What about Stalin? Are revolutions democratic? How can we have a planned economy? Is socialism still relevant?

Can socialism make sense?
An unfriendly dialogue

Sean Matgamna

With additional texts by Ernest Belfort Bax, August Bebel, Eugene Debs, Hal Draper, Albert Einstein, Frederick Engels, Henry Hyndman, Paul Lafargue, Vladimir Lenin, Rosa Luxemburg, David Marsland, Kenneth Minogue, William Morris, Roger Scruton, Max Shachtman, Martin Thomas, Leon Trotsky, and Clara Zetkin

Order for £14.80 including p&p from www.workersliberty.org/socialism.

Introduction

This pamphlet is a companion volume to Sean Matgamna's *Can Socialism Make Sense?* and the forthcoming *Why the Left is in Disarray*, which anatomises the political, ideological and moral crisis of the left. *Can Socialism Make Sense?* examines the arguments against socialism and the extra momentum they have gained in the era since the collapse of the old USSR and of Stalinism in Eastern Europe. It argues for the Marxist concept of socialism, as it was developed before Stalinism. In that concept democracy is pivotal, because only with extensive and responsive democracy can collective ownership of factories, office, logistics, communications, and other assets of social production be really collective.

So, how will that democracy emerge? How is it different from the parliamentary system which passes in conventional wisdom for the only democracy possible, and yet is seen by millions, with weary resignation, as a perpetual deception-machine? And what is the connection between that democracy and the agitation and activity which socialists do week in, week out — the demonstrations, strikes, occupations and so on which we support or organise?

To some readers this booklet may at first sight seem like an excursion into ancient history. It pivots on the debates in the labour movement about how to stop the onslaught which Margaret Thatcher led after 1979. Now we all know that Thatcher won in Britain, through defeating the 1984-5 miners' strike. Her similars and imitators won in other countries. The regime installed by Thatcher, now named "neo-liberalism", has become the established common sense.

Yet this is not an exercise in wistful might-have-beens. Of course the left is still a distance from the starting points we had in the early 1980s. Then, the trade unions had 12 million members and some 335,000 workplace reps; today, maybe six million and 150,000. Then, the 1980 Labour Party conference could open with a speech from the platform declaring that the next Labour government, "within a matter of days", would legislate to gain powers to nationalise by decree and "provide for industrial democracy".

This year, 2016, we have the Tory government saying that the junior doctors' dispute was "like the miners' strike" in that it threatened the authority of an elected government and could open floodgates for a wider working-class reassertion. And we have the startling surge in and into the Labour Party which gave left-winger Jeremy Corbyn a landslide victory in a leadership election initially considered a shoo-in for Labour's soft-right.

That is only a start. There will be more. The 2008 crash shattered all illusions that capitalism had reached a plateau, a Great Moderation. No bourgeois thinker tries to deny that future crashes of equal impact will come. Capitalism is inescapably crisis-ridden.

Capitalist policy is not on a smooth, steady path. Capital can inflict defeats, restructurings, dislocations on the working class, and sometimes — as with Thatcher — with long effects; but, by its very law of life, it must always reconstruct workforces, create new strategic confrontations. To advance, capital must exploit workers; to exploit workers, it must recruit them, assemble them, and throw itself into conflict with them. Sooner or later, this year or that year, and probably in forms and at times we do not expect, there will be new battles like those of the early 1980s.

This booklet argues for a liberating, extensive, economic-and-not-just-political democracy, as the essence of socialism and the working-class alternative to limited (in fact plutocratic) parliamentary democracy. That new democracy will not arise from classroom cogitations or seminars on different constitutional models, but from the methods and modes of organisation the working class develops, step by step, for the practical tasks of constructing its own struggles and winning control over its own economic circumstances. The early 1980s were a time for this sort of debate on democracy exactly because they were a time in which the needs of resistance to Thatcher made the development of methods and modes of organisation urgent business for tens of thousands of working-class activists.

The first section of this booklet includes the written debate in 1982 between Michael Foot, then Labour Party leader, and Sean Matgamna of Workers' Liberty (then *Socialist Organiser*). Matgamna's text here is expanded, as it was for a 1994 edition of the debate, and we also include the preface. The 1994 edition was produced for a public event that year in which Foot and Matgamna debated the same issues face-to-face. We include a report of that face-to-face debate.

The 1994 edition also included some appendices not reproduced here.

Foot's argument, in 1982 and 1994, was that the labour movement must be, before all else, democratic; that democracy meant self-confinement by the labour movement to parliamentary channels, institutions, and procedures; and that all strikes, demonstrations, mobilisations must

INTRODUCTION

be restrained by recognising the priority and authority of parliamentary channels.

The second section documents what the "extra-parliamentary" alternative denounced by Foot really was — what class-struggle socialists then grouped round *Socialist Organiser* were saying at the time. The final section gives us an obituary of Foot; and Foot describing Leon Trotsky as "in all history, the greatest man of action who was also a very great literary genius". When we debated Foot, we were not debating some deadbeat right-winger with no interest in left-wing words other than as "cover" and soft soap.

Martin Thomas, May 2016

Introduction to the web edition

When Michael Foot wrote articles in the *Observer* on democracy, revolution, socialism, and Stalinism, his immediate point was to insist that trade union direct action to resist the attacks of the Thatcher Government on the working class and the labour movement, would be a violation of democratic principle. Sean Matgamna wrote a reply, in a series of articles in *Socialist Organiser*.

Much was different in British politics then. The leaders of the Labour Party still promised to advance us towards socialism, saying only that their cautious parliamentary method was better than the militancy of the "extra-parliamentary left".

They still felt an obligation to debate politically with the activist left, instead of relying on Tory anti-union laws and authoritarian reworkings of Labour Party structures to repress us, as Blair does. Foot himself some years later, after he had retired from the Labour Party leadership, would debate the issues face-to-face with Sean Matgamna in a public meeting at Conway Hall, London, in 1994.

In 1982 there was an active Marxist-influenced left inside the Labour Party, only just starting to recede from its high tide in 1981. The Labour Party's debates and structures have shrivelled drastically since then, and most of those leftists, the AWL among them, now devote most of their efforts to activity outside those structures.

But the essentials of the debate are still relevant. Some of it — the reply to Foot's attempt to damn revolutionary socialism by equating it with Stalinism — is even more relevant now, in the aftermath of the collapse of Stalinism and its radical discrediting, than it was in 1982.

March 2007

Preface: Thatcherism and democracy

Socialism is impossible without democracy. You can not have collective ownership of the means of production without collective control, and collective control has by its nature to be democratic control. Collective ownership without democracy inevitably turns into the real ownership of the collectivised economy by those whose political power gives them control of it. This is an old, basic, socialist truth, reinforced by the experience of Stalin's counterfeit socialism in the USSR. Where there is no democracy, there will never be socialism. Socialists are democrats — or they are not socialists.

And because this is so — what follows?

Therefore, socialists should not advocate or promote direct action and illegal resistance against class legislation such as the Tory class law that hamstrings our trade unions because, by definition, such legislation has a parliamentary majority behind it?

Therefore, workers lose the right to resist injustice — like the poll tax, for example — when it is inflicted by a democratic parliament?

Therefore, the labour movement must repudiate the class struggle within democracy such as we have it in Britain, bourgeois democracy, by way of which the bourgeoisie rule in society and continue to exploit the working class?

Therefore, workers must always bow down low — as low as John Smith and his predecessors as Labour leader, Neil Kinnock and Michael Foot — before the parliamentary majority?

Or, on the contrary, is it possible for workers to reject this reasoning and fight back against a democratically elected parliamentary majority, and still remain democrats?

Is it possible without repudiating democracy for a labour movement to resist capitalist attack and class legislation, using direct action, and where necessary, illegal action, against an elected parliamentary majority government?

For example, millions of people refused to pay the poll tax; they defied the law, that is, they defied Parliament. It was their resistance that broke the poll tax and Mrs Thatcher. Yet that resistance, according to the Labour leaders, was nothing less than a crime against "democracy".

No matter how iniquitous a piece of class legislation may be, said Neil Kinnock and his friends — and they never denied that the poll tax was a piece of vicious class legislation — parliament must govern. No-one had the right to resist an anointed parliament!

These questions, in major and minor keys, were posed to the labour movement again and again throughout the 1980s.

In the early 1980s they were posed with great sharpness, and very great consequence. Having won the 1979 general election on a minority of the vote cast, the Tories launched a relentless many-pronged attack on the working class and the labour movement. Not since 1926 had there been in Britain so open a class-war government, or a government so willing to use every weapon necessary to beat workers down.

The Tories deliberately worsened the conditions of slump which began in 1980, the better to cut down the labour movement. Whole swathes of industry, and the militant labour organisations erected within them, were wiped out. Whole communities were devastated. A big part of a generation of young people was thrown out of industry and on to the scrap heap before they had had a real chance to begin to live.

The first of a long series of anti-union laws was put on the statute book, laws which by now add up to the most illiberal labour legislation in Western Europe. Under those laws, the British trade union movement can today be described at best as a semi-free labour movement.

The welfare state was undercut, the demolition of the National Health Service started. The Tories were sloughing off what was left of the post-war Tory-Labour-Liberal consensus and setting out on a radical bourgeois programme to reshape British society.

This minority-vote government used the state power ruthlessly.

Despite their cant about freeing people from state controls, the brutal use of state power was central to their entire project. Without it they could not have won.

To physically beat down striking workers during the 1984-5 miners' strike, they would organise the police as a semi-militarised force under the control of a national centre. Arbitrarily and illegally controlling the movements of miners, they sometimes acted quite outside the law. In 1986, they sent the police to strong-arm printworkers at Wapping on behalf of Rupert Murdoch.

When Thatcher started her drive against the working class, before mass unemployment had cut into the sinews of the labour movement, before so much of industry was destroyed, the labour movement still had the strength to challenge Thatcher and win. Before the 1982 Falklands war

Thatcher was as unpopular as she would again become by 1990, when the panicky Tory MPs dismissed her. Resistance by direct action was possible then, as in the 1970s, when Tory prime minister Heath was driven from office.

But was it democratically permissible? Did the labour movement have the democratic right to organise extraparliamentary resistance? Did it have the right to try to dislodge the Thatcher government by extra-parliamentary action?

Serious socialists — *Socialist Organiser*, for example — said: "Yes!" We advocated resistance and confrontation on every front possible, from industry to local government (where nominal left-wingers were strong) to parliament. We invoked the right of revolt and resistance to oppression and tyranny proclaimed by the serious bourgeois democrats who led the English revolution in the 17th century and the American and French revolutions in the 18th century. We argued for a fight by the labour movement to defend democracy against Thatcher's abuse of parliamentary power, and for a simultaneous fight, in the spirit of the old Chartists, to deepen and develop democracy.

The Labour establishment, its left and ex-left segment indistinguishable from the right, said: "No!". It is, they said, undemocratic to resist parliament. The Labour Party "hard left" — people like Ken Livingstone — said: "Yes! Resist!" but most of them soon thought better of it. In any case, as we will see, they did not resist.

It was the time of the great left-wing upsurge in the Labour Party, triggered by the comprehensive failure of Labour in government between 1974 and 1979. After the General Election defeat in mid-1979 the labour movement set out to draw the conclusions from over a decade of serious class struggle.

The left won a succession of victories at Labour Party conferences in Blackpool, Brighton, and Wembley. Such was the mood that Tony Benn was able to secure 83 per cent of the Constituency Labour Party votes when he stood against Denis Healey for deputy leader of the Labour Party. Our great weakness lay in our lack of organised forces in the trade unions.

It was possible, had the Labour Party and the trade unions challenged the Tories head on, to reforge the British working-class movement into a radical anti-capitalist force in the heat of the class struggle.

It was possible for the labour movement, defending the post-war welfare state, to have rallied the lower middle classes around itself. An eventual parliamentary majority for Labour policies is the least that might have been won.

That did not happen. The trade union leaders did not fight. Soon undercut by the slump. neither did the rank and file, to whom it had fallen in the 1960s and 70s to set the pace — not on the necessary scale, anyway.

The radicalisation was mainly a Labour Party affair — and a heavily lower-middle-class affair at that, often on "minority" and sectional issues. Symptomatically, the manifestos of even "very left wing" Labour Parties — Islington, for example — scarcely mentioned, or did not at all mention, the working class.

Nor did the local government left fight, in the early 1980s, when it mattered, when the Thatcher tide might still have been turned. Ken Livingstone's Greater London Council bottled out of a confrontation with the Tories, though that did not save the GLC. Lambeth stumbled into a sort of conflict in the mid-1980s; Liverpool, under Militant leadership, made some mobilisation in 1984, then did a deal with the Tories, leaving the miners in the lurch, and eventually stumbled into collapse.

The miners' battle of 1984-5 came very late. Yet it could have ignited the labour movement. With help from other workers at crucial turning points, the miners could have beaten Thatcher. If the dockers had struck for longer; if Liverpool council had gone for confrontation... Yet, in retrospect, it is not at all surprising that it did not go like that. It was too late. The Tories had become too strong. Thatcher looked unbeatable to a labour movement that had become seriously demoralised.

The Tories, seeing their enemy in unexpected disarray, gleefully improved on their early victories. Round after round of anti-union legislation was rammed through. The Thatcherites pushed the entire axis of British politics — and, slowly, the Labour Party too — to the right. Ultimately they hegemonised the Labour Party.

By the later 1980s, the Tories were like victorious cavalry riding around in command of a battlefield, looking for still-twitching targets. In 1989 they casually picked off and destroyed the National Dock Labour Scheme, something that no government would have risked contemplating a decade earlier. Now, the Labour Party scarcely dared even to protest.

The early 1980s was the decisive time. Large-scale resistance was possible then which later, for logistic, political and psychological reasons, became very difficult. Because of the slump, resistance to the Tories then would probably have had to be spurred and organised by a political campaign, developing a growing industrial dimension. That, for a while, seemed possible. When he defeated Denis Healey for Labour leader in 1980, Michael Foot promised to whip up such a "storm of indignation" against what the Tories were doing that they would again be driven from office as they had been driven out seven years before. It was what we needed.

But Foot never did it. He did not even try seriously. Instead, this long time Labour left winger who unexpectedly found himself leader of the Labour Party turned his fire on the serious Labour left, and thereby condemned himself to safe, in-house parliamentary posturing against the Tories.

His Labour Party left friends did the same. It was the onset of that frozen impotence so characteristic of the Labour Party leaders today — so strange and unnatural that even mainstream journalists, no, even the Liberals, can now sneer at Labour for its lack of fire against the Tories.

The future historians of the labour movement and of British politics will have to record the astonishing fact that when the Tories, using parliament as a base for the operations of a one-party minority dictatorship, were radically reshaping and diminishing British democracy — when they were curbing local government; destroying civil liberties; clawing back the hard-won rights of the labour movement, and many of the reforms it had achieved in 100 years of work; ruthlessly pushing through cranky bits of social engineering; wiping out much of Britain's industry and many millions of jobs — just at that time the leaders of the Labour Party, Michael Foot and his lame-brained understudy Neil Kinnock, were crusading in defence of democracy, not against the Tories, but against the Labour left! At exactly this point in Britain's political history the Labour leaders chose to crusade in defence of "democracy"... against their own left wing!

In parliament and in the big business newspaper, the *Observer*, Labour leader Michael Foot, concurring with the violent campaign of denunciation in the mainstream press, indicted the left as the main enemy of democracy, and branded it as an immediate threat! Those who threaten British democracy, said the political leaders of the labour movement while Thatcher was mercilessly grinding down the labour movement and destroying working-class rights, are those who want to use direct action to stop her!

The cry "democracy first" became the main ideological weapon in the drive by the Labour right and soft left, that is, the Labour establishment, to disarm the labour movement in face of the Tory onslaught.

"Democracy" was used to discredit the idea of direct action and banish it from consideration by the official labour movement. It was, inevitably, the issue on which the "soft left" separated itself finally from the more serious left. Later it was the blade of the knife the Labour establishment plunged into the back of the miners during their great strike. It has been the ultimate justification for craven inactivity all through the 1980s and well into the 90s. It was their "good", respect-worthy, public "reason" for a needless surrender to the Tories.

In the name of democracy they refused to defend democracy — the democratic rights of the labour movement, and of all British citizens! Without a struggle worthy of the name they surrendered British society to the rule of the rampant barbarians of new Toryism!

The history of reformist labour movements like the Labour Party includes many similar episodes, grim and obscene — such, for example, as the day in 1933 when the German Social Democratic leader Otto Wels, who had played a big part in the bloody suppression of the left in 1919, during which Karl Liebknecht and Rosa Luxemburg were killed, got up in the Reichstag and offered his party's loyal collaboration to the new, legally appointed and "democratic", Chancellor, Herr Hitler. It is their nature. When they kow-tow to the bourgeois establishment, they obey their deepest instincts!

They fear action against the bourgeoisie and they fear the rank and file. Yet there is more to it. The behaviour of the British Labour leaders in face of Thatcherism demands more explanation than is found in Marxist truisms about the general nature of reformism: reformist Labour leaders also come under the pressure of their members, and when their organisations are threatened, they sometimes try to defend them. Even the most wretched creatures defend themselves when driven into a corner, when they can no longer fool themselves into thinking that things will turn out all right. The great mystery of Britain's labour and trade union leaders in 1980 and after is that they did not do that. They did not even try to do it.

Trade union organisations which had seemed as powerful as the Labour government itself in the mid-70s sank away into political nothingness before the first attacks of an enemy they could probably have beaten had they fought. Why?

To look for one simple explanation for that behaviour is probably misleading. Yet I want to highlight one part of the explanation, which Michael Foot's ruminations bring out pretty clearly in the articles reprinted in this pamphlet.

At the beginning of the 1980s, the Labour and trade union leaders were terrified of a campaign of direct action to resist Thatcher because —

to use the phrase Michael Foot used in his *Observer* article — they feared "the stormtroopers".

They feared to resist Thatcher because they feared a military coup in Britain.

They were far from confident that democracy in Britain was stable. Despite what they said in their demagogic denunciations of the left, they knew that the ruling class which Thatcher led was prepared to try to smash British democracy if that was the only way they could win against the working class movement which they were determined to beat down.

They knew, having been in government, how close British democracy had come to a breakdown in the mid-1970s. They drew lessons from the military coup which the armed forces in Chile had made against a socialist government, in September 1973.

Behind all their confident assertions about British democracy lived the fear and terror of men and women who felt that they had looked into the abyss in the mid-1970s. This comes through plainly in Michael Foot's *Observer* pieces, reprinted here. To understand what happened in the early 80s you need to look at what happened in 1973.

Nineteen seventy-three was a year of great class struggle in Britain. It came to a climax with the miners' strike and an unscheduled General Election in February 1974, called by Tory Prime Minister Edward Heath to answer the question: "who runs Britain — the Government or the unions?". The Tories lost.

A tremendously militant labour movement had taken on the Tories and driven them from office. But the right-wing-led Labour Party was the political beneficiary. It formed a government, backed by the trade unions and the whole working-class movement.

It was heavily dependent on that movement and it made various concessions to it. It scrapped the anti-union laws the Tories had put on the statute book.

But, over time, the Labour government — actively backed by the "left-wing" union leaders, without whose support it could not have governed — turned on its supporters, using as its weapon a "social contract" which undercut militancy and worked ultimately to serve the interests of the employers.

The Labour Party had fought the election on a programme of "bringing about a fundamental redistribution of wealth and power in the interests of working people". Even the colourful right-winger Denis Healey had talked about squeezing the rich "until the pips squeak". People had voted Labour on that basis.

Now, Labour in government slowly put the squeeze on the working class, beginning a process of undermining the self-confidence of the workers: it would have catastrophic consequences after 1979, when the Tories came back to power and used the slump to beat down and half-crush the labour movement.

What happened in the mid-1970s could not have happened in that way if the leaders of the trade union movement — some of them left-wingers with reasonable credentials, like Jack Jones of the TGWU — had not, because they feared an all-out clash with the ruling class, decided to scale down their demands and deliver the labour movement up to collaboration with the Government and the capitalists.

It was, on a much bigger scale and with Labour in government, curiously like an incident in 1919, which Aneurin Bevan tells of in his book, *In Place of Fear*. The story was told to him by Robert Smillie.

"Lloyd George sent for the labour leaders, and they went, so Robert told me, 'truculently determined they would not be talked over by the seductive and eloquent Welshman'. At this Bob's eyes twinkled in his grave, strong face. 'He was quite frank with us from the outset,' Bob went on. 'He said to us: "Gentlemen, you have fashioned, in the Triple Alliance of the unions represented by you, a most powerful instrument. I feel bound to tell you that in our opinion we are at your mercy. The army is disaffected and cannot be relied upon. Trouble has occurred already in a number of camps. We have just emerged from a great war and the people are eager for the reward of their sacrifices, and we are in no position to satisfy them. In these circumstances, if you carry out your threat and strike, then you will defeat us.

"'But if you do so,' went on Mr Lloyd George, 'have you weighed the consequences? The strike will be in defiance of the government of the country and by its very success will precipitate a constitutional crisis of the first importance. For, if a force arises in the state which is stronger than the state itself, then it must be ready to take on the functions of the state, or withdraw and accept the authority of the state. Gentlemen', asked the Prime Minister quietly, 'have you considered, and if you have, are you ready?' From that moment on, said Robert Smillie, 'we were beaten and we knew we were'." (Aneurin Bevan, *In Place of Fear*, London, 1952, pp.20-21)

Was the threat of a military takeover serious? Very serious, it seems. Lord Carver, the army's Chief of Staff at the time, later publicly admitted that there had been talk of a military coup in Britain among "fairly senior" officers.

"Fairly senior officers were ill-advised enough to make suggestions that perhaps, if things got terribly bad, the army would have to do something about it..."

The left union leaders, Hugh Scanlon of the AEU and former Spanish Civil War volunteer Jack Jones, like their MP equivalents and fellow-travellers such as Michael Foot, had long insisted in labour movement debates that, yes, you could have a peaceful socialist revolution in Britain; yes, of course, parliament was stable and democracy safe in the hands of Britain's generals and admirals.

Now they looked at recent events in Chile where, in September 1973, a military coup had destroyed one of the oldest democracies in the world. Facing the realities of class power and class struggle in Britain, knowing that if the working-class movement pushed ahead then it risked a savage Chile-style backlash, what did they do? Did they admit that they had been wrong all those years about the reliability of parliamentary democracy? Did they warn the labour movement? Did they tell workers to prepare to fight?

No. Terrified by their own industrial and political victory over the Tories, they turned and ran, demobilising the labour movement and disarming it before the Tories. The ultimate price we paid for this was Thatcherism.

The Labour and trade union leaders confronted the new Thatcher government in a blue funk at the possible consequences of a new round of 1970s level class struggle. So, over time, cumulatively, they surrendered.

The ruling class in Britain did not need to resort to a coup. That was one of the things that Foot was signalling to them by turning on the left, as he did. Yet the working class in Britain, missing the tide in 1974-79, nonetheless suffered a series of terrible defeats.

It has been pinioned and disabled by hostile Tory laws. We lost the recent strike at Timex because Tory law cripples solidarity action.

The British labour movement experienced no mass bloodletting. But it has experienced an awful debilitation in the Thatcher years and after. The French used to call the tropical prison on Devil's Island, "the dry guillotine": Thatcherism was to Pinochet's coup what the dry guillotine was to the one which chops off your head.

The astonishing failure of the Labour and trade union establishment, powerful politicians, so recently in government, and powerful leaders of great trade unions, recently in strong partnership with government, even to defend their own immediate interests in the early 1980s, thus was a late by-product of the bitter class struggles of the first half of the 1970s.

The consequences are still with them — and with us. They gutted themselves even as reformists. Part of the Labour leaders' mid-70s scuttling was the Labour government's decision to initiate cuts in the social services, in 1976, at the dictat of the IMF. They thereby opened the epoch of cuts, paving the way for Tory victory in the 1979 election, and for the savage cuts the Tories then embarked upon, and for Labour's own collapse before them. Labour in office set the Tory bandwagon rolling, and then fell under its wheels!

The central failure of the Labour leaders in the 80s and 90s has been a profound failure of reformist nerve, a moral buckling and bowing down before the capitalists' right to rule and the dog eat dog philosophy according to which they rule. Today official Labour does not even dare proclaim, let alone fight for, the democratic principle embodied in the Health Service Nye Bevan created in 1948: the democratic right to equality in health care, the inalienable right to life and an equal medical right to remain alive and in good health for everyone, and not only for the rich.

When the Tories say — and it is now one of their central arguments — that modern state-of-the-art health care is too expensive to give to everyone, that is, to the poor, and so can only be made available to those who have the money to pay for it, they deny that principle.

Even the reformist leaders of the 1940s would have responded to such Tory ideas as people stung to action in defence of their most basic beliefs in human equality and social solidarity. But they were convinced reformists. The present leaders are not even reformists. They accept the gruesome Tory argument that "we" cannot afford proper health care for the poor in a society which spends vast millions on arms, makes tax cuts to benefit the wealthy, and devotes immense amounts of wealth to sustain the upper classes! They only ask the Tories to go about things with a little less savagery. The Tories have not obliged them.

It is only momentarily surprising that those who in the 80s sacrificed the labour movement on the altar of "democracy" should fail so utterly to react even as democrats to the Tories' open denial of human equality in one of its most basic terms — the right to life. For the Health Service now as for all the issues of the 80s, serious commitment to democracy is either a commitment to fight for democracy, or else, in class society, it is just time-serving waffle.

One way to put the issues discussed in this pamphlet into perspective is to examine two events in the industrial struggle of the 1980s. Remember, according to the Labour leaders as we faced the Thatcherite onslaught, that direct action against a parliamentary majority, against its government, or against its police, is the greatest crime against democracy; it is the crime characteristic above all else of revolutionary socialists. Legality at all costs is better. So say the reformists. Look at the experience.

In 1989 dockers struck in defence of the National Dock Labour Scheme, which had regulated labour in the ports for the previous 40 years. When the workers were already out, nineteen shop stewards, the leaders of the strike at Tilbury, were sacked.

Circumstances were very unfavourable to the dockers; their strike soon crumbled: the National Dock Labour Scheme, one of the great achievements of the post-war Labour government, was abolished.

The sacking of the nineteen Tilbury stewards was a great blow, maybe a shattering blow, against the 1989 dockers' strike.

Two years later, an industrial tribunal said it was "unfair dismissal". Twelve of the nineteen have got their jobs back; the seven chief "troublemakers" are not likely to get back theirs. But even if all nineteen were to be reinstated, the effects of these ruthless, "unfair" dismissal — blows struck by the employers and the government to defeat the striking dockers — can never be undone: the debilitating dismissals worked their effects on the dockers' movement in 1989, and that is irrevocable.

Or take the "Battle of Orgreave", a turning point in the great miners' strike.

At Orgreave coke works near Sheffield, in the summer of 1984, Mrs Thatcher's police — semi-militarised and organised for strikebreaking from a special national police centre — fought miners' pickets in one of the major battles of the strike. If the miners had won Orgreave, they would probably have won the strike.

The police, specially trained and equipped, and operating like an army, won. They won by sheer brute, ruthless force, and more than they needed of it.

As has already been said, much that the police did during the miners' strike was widely criticised at the time, even by liberals, for example, illegally stopping people moving freely about the country, or "occupying" pit villages. Still, they did it.

They did everything they needed to do to win. So did the vast employer-government machine for making dirty propaganda against the miners, whose main stock-in-trade was denunciation of "violence" — miners' violence.

And they won. If Orgreave was one of the turning points in the miners' strike, the miners' strike was a turning point for the working class and the labour movement. After the miners, strike, stone-age employers all over Britain were greatly strengthened.

Even so, say the philosophic people who lead the Labour Party and the TUC, it was a victory for law and order and parliamentary government against a semi-insurrectionary working-class movement. Democracy and the rule of law must prevail.

Move on seven years after the miners' strike.

In June 1991, 35 miners were paid a total of £500,000 in compensation for damage and injuries they received during the battles at Orgreave.

Earlier — in 1985 — the cases against some 95 miners charged with offences at Orgreave collapsed, when police notes were found to be forged.

But no, the courts cannot order a replay of the Battle of Orgreave. They can not, even if they would, order the Coal Board to go back seven years and act as if the miners had won at Orgreave; they can not turn Britain's industrial and political life back seven years, wiping out the still continuing effects of the miners' defeat, and substituting for it the effects of a miners' victory. If that were likely to follow from the ruling, the court would have reached a different verdict, or delayed giving one for another seven years.

Force decided that battle, which itself decided so much for the labour movement. The crying pity of it is that we did not manage to mobilise enough force to beat Thatcher's cossacks off the field at Orgreave!

The class struggle is not conducted, least of all by the employers, who always have enormous advantages, according to the Queensberry rules for boxing or by the Parliamentary Rules of Debate.

There are no instant replays in the class struggle! The winners keep the spoils. They will keep the spoils until we, having learned these lessons, beat them in the inevitable next round of the struggle of the classes, the ceaseless struggle which will never end until the working class, the great mass of the people, win the battle of political and social democracy.

In the face of Thatcher, *Socialist Organiser* advocated direct action and defiance of the Tories all across the fronts of the class struggle: industrial direct action, local government resistance, parliamentary withdrawal of co-operation. We said to the labour movement: fight the Tories by every means possible, or face a historic defeat. Our comrades were active in the trade unions, and in the Labour Party, advocating such policies.

We initiated the Rank and File Mobilising Committee for Labour Democracy, which united most of the left in the drive that, for a while before the labour movement and especially the unions were ground down by the Thatcherites, took the Labour Party sharply to the left.

We argued that the labour movement should fight to kick out the Tories and replace them with a "workers' government", a Labour government radically different from all previous Labour governments, doing for the working class the sort of things Thatcher spent the 1980s doing for the bourgeoisie.

We fought the passivity of the right and the soft left; we criticised the empty radicalism of the local government left who surrendered to the Tories by pursuing a policy of Labour council business-as-usual, disguised with left-wing verbal trimmings and grants for good "minority" causes. Fighting the class struggle was not on their "agenda".

A central part of that work was to oppose the craven mystifications about democracy with which the soft left rationalised their surrender to the Tories and the Labour right, and began their own slide to the right. Sharing in our own way, and from a pre-Stalin Marxist point of view, the broad labour movement's commitment to democracy as an irreplaceable element of socialism, to which Foot, Kinnock and their friends demagogically and dishonestly appealed, we challenged the ideas put out by Foot and Kinnock and *Tribune* from within the democratic tradition that they falsely claimed and misrepresented. We insisted that commitment to democracy does not rule out direct action and direct, immediate resistance to oppression.

We explained the genuine tradition of working-class democracy and the real history of the struggle for democracy, first by "the people" led by the bourgeoisie, and then by the labour movement.

We contrasted the unrealised goals of that struggle for democracy with both the ideas of the anti-democrats posing as socialists, the Stalinists and various Stalinoid "Trotskyists", and the anti-socialists (like Foot and Kinnock) posing, in essence falsely, as serious democrats. We insisted that Britain does not have "democracy", but *bourgeois* democracy. Real democracy — self-rule in our lives, including economic self-rule — is yet to be won and must be fought for.

Faced with Thatcher, the only real democrats, we argued, were those who were willing to fight for democracy, even against a parliamentary majority. But those of us who advocated the class struggle were increasingly marginalised as the decade wore on.

In the broad labour movement, the Kinnockites won the argument. The Tories, the trade union bureaucrats, and the local government left who postured, gestured and prattled instead of mobilising workers for a necessary fight, won it for them.

These craven "democrats", who took their stand against the direct-action left as defenders of democracy, have run before the Tories down through a whole decade and a half during which they never dared stand and fight the Government which has attacked and undermined democracy as well as attacking and socially undermining the working class.

Knowing exactly what was going on in the miners' strike, not only did they fail to defend the miners against Thatcher and her police (who often acted illegally), they joined in the hypocritical howling against the "violence" of miners struggling against savage capitalist economic, social, political and police violence.

They arrived at the April 1992 general election spiritually so battered that they did not even dare to promise to restore the democratic rights the Tories have cut out of our trade unionism.

The labour movement after 1979 was faced with a choice of either prevailing over the Tories or of accepting savage defeat. Foot and his friends did not, and could not, choose the status quo ante. Defeat following surrender in the interests of "preserving democracy" brought the destruction of a wide array of our democratic rights, and brought deep demoralisation and self doubt to the labour movement.

Not to fight brought many of the worst consequences that defeat, even a defeat involving the army, would have brought. We have learned that, in a decade and a half of Tories lording it brutally over a weak and intimidated opposition and over a working class more powerless than it had been since the 1930s.

The class struggle is a fact of life: you can not evade its consequences by running from it. Running from it is only another way of losing it. To prattle, as Labour's leaders did and do, about classless "democracy", is to fight on behalf of the ruling class in the battle of ideas which is so central a part of the class struggle.

The material in this pamphlet in reply to Michael Foot first appeared in *Socialist Organiser* at the beginning of 1982. It has been reorganised and expanded; the political line has not been altered in any way — for instance, what is said about how a Marxist Workers' Government should respond to losing an election is as it was in the January 1982 text; so is the description and characterisation of the USSR.

We believe that the labour movement must again take up the fight for democracy, not only to regain what Thatcher and her friends took from us in the form of trade union rights, local democracy and civil liberties, but to extend democracy in the direction the pioneers of the labour movement — the Chartists — wanted to go.

I hope the discussions in this collection will stimulate thought on this question and maybe help convince the labour movement militants that they should join us in the fight against the Tories and their right-wing Labour political spawns and understudies, and fight for democracy as it was understood by its pioneers — social democracy, which in modern conditions can only be socialism.

Sean Matgamna, 1994

Michael Foot's article was published in *The Observer,* 10 and 17 January 1982. Sean Matgamna's response was written in 1982 and an expanded version of it was published in the 1994 pamphlet, *Socialism and Democracy.*

The debate:
My kind of democracy

Michael Foot

Why Parliament? Can those old arthritic limbs still move as the nation needs? Why parliamentary democracy? Why should democratic socialists and, more especially, democratic socialists in Britain, continue to assert their faith in the supremacy of Parliament? Were those who framed the Labour Party constitution right in their sense of balance when they declared that their objective was to sustain a Labour Party in Parliament and in the country?

These questions touch some of the present discontents within the party, and it is right that the answers should be sought afresh. It is not possible or desirable that the socialist acceptance of parliamentary institutions should be automatic or uncritical or unqualified.

Aneurin Bevan was fond of insisting that the democratic case for the British parliament was of quite recent derivation; only since 1929, the first House of Commons in which he sat, had its authority been founded on universal suffrage. Moreover, some of the most astringent pages he ever wrote were directed to the question of what would happen if the democratic parliament failed to challenge capitalist power effectively.

However, he also showed, in practice, in deed even more colourfully than in word, how the institution could be used for truly socialist purposes, both here and now and in the fulfilment of longer, idealistic aims. At one period, in his youth, he had flirted with syndicalist ideas, as did many South Wales miners of that generation. But, increasingly, as the years passed, he placed his confidence in collectivist, socialist power, to be wielded by the central state, acting through parliament, with all the devices, chances and protections of open debate which he knew so well how to exploit on behalf of his people and his party.

So his authority can be invoked to dismiss any suggestion that parliament, the British parliament, can or should be reduced to a subordinate role. And one purpose of this essay will be to show, to prove, that there are paramount reasons, in the interests of socialism, why the Labour Party needs to use parliament more ambitiously and deliberately than ever before.

As I write these words, something else, the most agonising event of the time, the suppression of all free opinion and institutions in Poland, presses for attention, and it is by no reckoning irrelevant to our own argument about parliamentary institutions. The failures — and the accompanying horrors — of Soviet Communism both in Poland and the Soviet Union itself, are in part due to the apparent incapacity of the centralised Soviet state to develop or protect genuine, independent institutions of almost any kind. And the Communist answers to this charge are devoid of any content whatever. Their most persuasive apologists have never been able to explain how the enormities of Stalinism happened — or what guarantee there can be that they should never develop again.

Whenever these important theoretical fields are explored anew, one path must point to the necessity of establishing some truly independent parliamentary institutions. No doubt this is another course which the trade unions formed in Solidarity in Poland would have wished to have pursued, and why not? Trade union power, as we have frequently witnessed in our own history, needs the buttress of legislative protection. Trade union power alone cannot provide a sufficient substitute for a free, independent, central state power.

As the British people, along with many others across our anxious planet, mark events in Poland, they are not likely, whatever their criticisms of the present Westminster parliament and its occupants, to extend their anger and frustration to a condemnation of parliament altogether. Indeed, an opposite development is much more probable. Whatever its other manifold deficiencies, parliament can still symbolise the attempt to settle disputes by better methods than brute force. Any democratic socialists who overlooked that connection would hardly deserve the name.

However, no topical and terrible illustration from Poland is needed to clinch the case. With or without it, there is plentiful proof on our own doorsteps of the proposition that for socialists — for those who accept that only by profound socialist change can the deeper disease of our society be cured — the dominant need is to turn the nation's mind to parliamentary action.

Such an attitude is demanded, not by some ancient allegiance to musty constitutional theories, but in the name of common human decency — in the interests, for example, of the people of Ebbw Vale, Tredegar and Rhymney, my constituents, where the unemployment total has more than doubled in the past two and a half years to an horrific 22 per cent, and still rises, and where these growing congregations of unemployed families are having their means of livelihood cut and cut again. How are they, like the millions in our country who suffer the same afflictions, to be rescued?

Trade union power cannot save us, particularly since, at such a perilous time, the trade unions are compelled to conduct defensive, rearguard battles. During the last great slump of the 1930s trade union membership was more than cut in half; the total fell to less than three and a half million in the early 1930s, whereas in the late 1920s it had risen to more than eight million. No comparable calamity has befallen the trade union movement in this slump of the 1980s, but the fall in membership resulting from mass unemployment has forced one union after another to apply protective measures.

In consequence, some of the worst effects of the slump have been warded off by individual unions, or the terms of redundancy have been improved, or the unions themselves have been able to guard their capacity to resist another day. But the notion that the unions, in these threatened circumstances, can suddenly acquire a vastly augmented power, sufficient to shape the whole scene, is a delusion.

What they do have, if they husband their strength properly, is the power, quite legitimately and constitutionally, to exploit the mistakes of our opponents, and to be ready for the moment when political victory may be extracted from an industrial conflict.

This is what the miners did in 1974, when Edward Heath took the arrogant gamble of trying to use a General Election to win a constitutional battle against people engaged strictly in an industrial dispute. The experience is instructive: it is worth recalling that the miners, both in the 1972 strike and the 1974 strike, had massive public support behind them, arising partly from the way their comparative wage rates had been cut over the previous two decades. It is also worth recalling that their victory, for its full harvest to be garnered, required political and parliamentary action alongside the industrial victories.

The legislation carried through parliament in the wake of the 1945 victory was extensive both for the miners and the rest of the unions, and the labour movement as a whole, and the nation.

The miners secured a good pay settlement, an entirely new departure in government assistance to secure a settlement for pneumoconiosis victims and above all, the acceptance of the "Plan for Coal", the first real planning agreement between the government and the unions and the Coal Board, which has provided the cornerstone for the industry ever since, and on the continued fulfilment of which the union still adamantly insists.

All these achievements required parliamentary action. The unions generally secured advances hardly less considerable, even if some of them have proved more difficult to sustain in the new circumstances. But, again, it must be emphasised, parliamentary action was required to repeal the Tory Industrial Relations Act and to extend trade union rights and protection to many millions of people previously uncovered under the Health and Safety legislation, or the special legislation which sought to extend new rights and benefits to women — the biggest reforms ever secured in this field in any parliament since women first won the vote.

Tragically, many of these advances over a wide field have been deliberately turned back by the Tories in the past three years or, more insidiously, their effectiveness has been destroyed by mass unemployment. None the less, indeed all the more, the absolute necessity of parliamentary action to ensure and safeguard industrial advance is underlined.

What the parliamentary action of the 1974-79 period also accomplished, despite the setbacks, was to produce conditions in which trade union membership rose to a higher figure than ever before and trade union participation in the whole wide process of industrial decision-making was carried further than ever before. And that was good for the country, too.

Some of the worst effects of the 1973-75 slump were warded off, for the unions and the whole nation, just as, given similar common action between the government and the unions, the worst effects of the 1979-81 slump could have been warded off. The risk would have been a good deal more manageable had we used properly the inestimable advantage of Britain's acquisition of North Sea oil between the two slump periods.

What should have happened in the late 1970s and what should happen in the middle 1980s, is the logical development of the intelligent government-union collective action of the 1974-76 period. We need a new major thrust forward across the whole of industry in the field of industrial democracy, with the authoritative engagement of trade unionists of all kinds and at all levels in the improvement of production and distribution of wealth for themselves, their industries and services and the community as a whole.

That will largely depend on the decisions of the unions themselves; but parliamentary action and a parliamentary majority will also be needed for the purpose. It was the prospective gains in industrial democracy which proved the most severe casualty of the loss of our real parliamentary majority in 1976. We still stayed in office after that date, quite rightly in my opinion, to try to protect the gains already secured, and to ward off the worst perils of the Tory counter-revolution, the likely horrors of which were already visible. But it is necessary to recall some of the next pressing items on our agenda which were blocked. They reappear on the present agenda of talks between the representatives of the Labour Party and the TUC, and they will surely occupy a prominent place in the party's next election manifesto.

We shall rightly resume the unfinished business of 1976 in the field of industrial democracy, and we shall need a full parliamentary majority for the purpose. It will have to be a Labour majority, for both in the field of industrial relations and of industrial democracy it is clear enough that the Social Democrats *[SDP, a party which split from Labour in 1981, merging with the Liberals to form the "Liberal Democrats" in 1988]*, like the Liberals, are deeply hostile to trade union rights.

But, it may be insisted, am I not pushing at an open door or erecting an Aunt Sally of my own design? Who in the labour movement, who on the left, even the so-called hard left, opposes parliamentary action? Of course it is needed. The real question concerns extra parliamentary action which may be the necessary handmaiden, the indispensable ally, of parliamentary action. Is that not a more profitable field of scrutiny?

Should we not be seeking new and more effective methods of extra-parliamentary action, drawing some lessons from the past maybe, from Wat Tyler, the Levellers, the Chartists, the Suffragettes, all of whom did certainly engage in extra-parliamentary activity, and to some considerable effect?

Since Tony Benn in particular has cited these examples in recent months, presumably to point their appositeness to modern circumstances, it is worth pausing for a moment to mention that all such analogies are out of focus and therefore misleading.

Wat Tyler had no representative to whom he could put his case, not even a witenagemot where he could stage a mass lobby. The men of Cromwell's armies, including the Levellers, did represent a much larger total of the British people of that century than the parliament which Cromwell first saved with his sword and then shut down when it proved obstreperous: so there were good democratic grounds for his action in both instances.

As for the Chartists, they argued long and most instructively about the means by which they could establish parliamentary rights and, more especially, how extensive should be the franchise they wished to secure. Their declared aim was to establish a parliament which they could trust, not one they wished to bypass. Extra-parliamentary action was imperative since they had no effective voice inside; actually to win the voice inside was the aim. Of course, to achieve such results, it was necessary to take action outside parliament, and with every justice.

Even so, they argued passionately about the way they should proceed in the classic debate between the advocates of moral force and physical force. "Whatever is gained in England by force, by force must be sustained, but whatever springs from knowledge and justice will sustain itself" — such was the brave and famous statement of that case by William Lovett, and before the declaration is dismissed as too romantic or idealistic, let no one forget that his greatest "physical force" opponent, Julian Harney, came to describe William Lovett as "the first in honour among the Chartists".

And the Suffragettes, like the Chartists, resorted to legal or sometimes illegal action outside parliament precisely because they too were denied the right to speak and act inside parliament. It is an irony that they should now be paraded as the opponents of parliamentary methods.

There are such opponents, of course, real ones with a theory to sustain them, who hold it as an essential part of their creed that parliament is a fake and a fraud, a distraction from the real means whereby power in the state may be captured. This idea cannot properly and precisely be defined as Marxist, since Karl Marx never applied his full genius to the problem. He seems just to have assumed — and why not? — that in the democratic state which might mark a phase before the full achievement of his own brand of Communism, there would be an elected national assembly — in other words, a parliament.

Karl Marx and Friedrich Engels also seemed to envisage that in England (partly in view of the existence of the still undemocratic parliament of those times) there might be a peaceful transition to socialism. Towards the end of his life Engels (so often presented as the foremost military expert by Marxists) became more and more convinced of the dangers and futility of the resort to force and not merely in semi-democratic England.

He began to glimpse the same hope in France and Germany: "The parties of order, as they call themselves, perish because of the legal conditions set up by themselves. With Odilon Barrot they cry out in despair *la légalité nous tue* — legality is our death — while we with the same legality acquire swelling muscles and red cheeks and look the picture of health. And if we are not insane enough to favour them by letting them drive us into street battles... "

Engels's warning might well be studied by those self-styled revolutionaries who speak today too readily of the resort to illegal methods or to street battles. Those who think socialism is to be won there should at least train to become soldiers or policemen — to face the storm troopers.

Both Lenin and Trotsky did apply their brilliant and ruthless intellects to the problems which Marx and Engels had at least side-stepped, and these two, together or apart, poured pitiless scorn on the parliamentary institutions they knew best. They thought perhaps that other parliaments might be as futile or obstructive for their purposes as the Russian Duma. They, or some of their followers, made the mistake of imagining that the British parliament was fashioned in that same mould.

But it would be foolish to attribute the same mistake to Trotsky. He would never have been guilty of the infantile, querulous condemnations of parliament and parliamentary action which some of his self-styled followers adopt. Karl Marx once remarked playfully that he could hardly call himself a Marxist, and Trotsky, the foremost literary genius brought forth by the Soviet revolution, would surely have disowned, with one sweep of his pen, the whole breed of modern Trotskyists.

So far this is a small part of the case. A respectable Marxist or near Marxist doctrine, and one with an ever-recurrent relevance to modern conditions, one which offers some response to human nature itself, is that which describes the catastrophic or apocalyptic view of human development — the prophecy of a great, supreme crisis as the inexorable means of establishing the new society, as opposed to the steady, remorseless, Fabian method of human advancement.

National and international moods reflecting different attitudes to this great argument have tended to change (true to the Marxist theory) as economic conditions themselves have changed. For example, the full Marxist interpretation was highly approved in most socialist theoretical discussion in the 1930s, while the Fabian alternative of "the inevitability of gradualness" was dismissed as little better than a form of treachery.

During the post-1945 period, however, when Fabian methods seemed to show some success in practice, the theoretical boot was transferred to the other foot, and the change-over was wondrously enshrined in the writings of John Strachey. His masterly expositions of the 1930s stated the apocalyptic case more conclusively than ever before, while his masterly expositions of the 1950s stated the Fabian or democratic socialist case more convincingly than any other writings in English in the same period.

However, with the collapse of the post-1945 economic order, in the Western world as a whole and in Britain in particular during the 1970s, it is not surprising that the Marxist arguments of the Thirties should have acquired a new vogue and validity, or, to interpolate one personal recollection, that Tony Benn should have sought to enlighten the members of the 1976 Callaghan Cabinet with a circulation of the minutes of the Macdonald cabinet of 1930-31.

And, for further measure, we may compare the disillusion which spread throughout the labour movement after 1931 — a deep doubt about the democratic process itself and, especially, the parliamentary process — with the form and scale of disillusion which spread after the 1979 defeat. There were, and remain, likenesses between the two, although, as I shall hope to show, the dissimilarities are crucial.

Yet this recital of dates or authorities is not intended in any sense to reduce the gravity of the argument. Of course this particular Marxist claim has an abiding strength, and any socialist who spurned it would be a fool. Indeed, the classic application of the doctrine in the 1930s, more telling than anything written by the orthodox Marxists themselves, was made by the most eminent and respected theoretician of the Labour Party — almost the last of the species — by R H Tawney.

He wrote (in 1934) his verdict on how the Labour government of 1929-31 "had crawled slowly to its doom", and almost every sentence retains his ferocious resonance: "What was tried, and found wanting, was, in short, not merely two years of a Labour cabinet, but a decade of Labour politics... The fundamental question, as always, is: Who is to be master?

"Is the reality behind the decorous drapery of political democracy to continue to be the economic power wielded by a few thousand — or, if that be preferred, a few hundred thousand — bankers, industrialists, and land-owners? Or shall a serious effort be made — as serious, for example, as was made, for other purposes, during the war — to create organs through which the nation can control, in co-operation with other nations, its economic destinies; plan its business as it deems most conducive to the general well-being; override, for the sake of economic efficiency, the obstruction of vested interests; and distribute the product of its labours in accordance with some generally recognised principles of justice?

Capitalist parties presumably accept the first alternative. A Socialist Party chooses the second. The nature of its business is determined by its choice."

Tawney (having soaked himself in Marxism) presented the challenge in near-Marxist terms, and he concentrated it all in an immortal phrase which Marx would have envied: "Onions can be eaten leaf by leaf, but you cannot skin a live tiger paw by paw... If the Labour Party is to tackle its job with some hope of success, it must mobilise behind it a body of conviction as resolute and informed as the opposition in front of it." In other words, Tawney, the great social democrat, to apply the term properly instead of the modern defilement, recognised the existence of the class struggle and the mighty convulsions required to secure its exorcism.

How to attempt to answer — or even to seek a mitigation of — a case so indisputable? To do so may appear just foolhardy. For has not Tawney ranged himself on the side of those who damn not merely the Labour practitioners of parliamentarianism, but the process itself?

Yet the effort must be made, for there are in my judgement profound reasons why socialists in the 1980s, if they are to serve their cause truly (and, as important as the cause itself, the people who march with us), must show a deeper insight and wisdom than the socialists of the 1930s were able to prescribe. After all, we should have learnt something from half a century of such tumult and terror in human affairs.

And part of what we have learnt, or should have learnt, adds up to a direct refutation of apocalyptic Marxism, or, if you wish, a justification, in a quite different sense from the old one, of the inevitability of gradualness. Throughout these years, several different rivers of experience merge into the same torrent. I ask for the readers' patience as I explore a few of them.

Off and on during these past two and a half years since Labour's electoral defeat of May 1979, Goldsmith's famous lines have floated incongruously through my mind:

When lovely woman stoops to folly
And finds too late that men betray
What charm can soothe her melancholy,
What art can wash her guilt away?

And political parties subjected to such outrages are even more difficult to soothe. It may be a slight comfort to recall that the condition is not unprecedented.

The same R H Tawney was the leading expert on Labour's post-1931 condition: "British socialists," he wrote, "frequently conduct themselves as though the most certain method of persuading the public to feel complete confidence in their cause were to convince it that they feel no confidence in each other. They draw their controversial knives at the first cross-roads they can encounter which, if suicide is the object of their demonstrations — it is often the effect — is undoubtedly the right place to choose for the purpose."

And again, even more directly: "After the collapse of 1931, an epidemic of the 'infantile disease of leftism' was obviously overdue. It raged for some months like measles in Polynesia, and set thousands gibbering. Private Socialisms flourished. There were absurd exhibitions of self-righteous sectarianism by cliques thanking God — or the latest improvement of him — that they were not as their benighted neighbours."

But stop. Tawney can be quoted for ever, and there is one more, of even greater appositeness, to come, and to guide us in answer to his own apparently inescapable challenge.

In 1934, in that matchless philippic against the 1931 Labour Cabinet, he was writing before he and most others had examined the full nature of Soviet totalitarianism. It is certainly doubtful whether he would have moderated the ferocity of his invective on that account; indeed, it might have been reinforced by the fear that a fresh democratic Socialist failure would help open the gates to totalitarianism.

But certainly too he would not — and did not — condone those horrors in any sense whatever or attempt to burke the necessity to put the case for democracy. On the contrary, he wrote (in 1953): "The fact remains that the prizes, however glittering, won by way of totalitarianism, are rarely those which they sought. The means destroy the end... The truth is that a conception of Socialism which views it as a power, on which all else depends, is not, to speak with moderation, according to light. The question is not merely whether the State owns and controls the means of production. It is also who owns and controls the State. It is not certain, though it is probable, that Socialism can in England be achieved by the methods proper to democracy. *It is certain that it cannot be achieved by any other.*" The italics are mine; but Tawney writing today would certainly have accepted the emphasis.

The argument about ends and means has persisted ever since the idea of establishing a Socialist Commonwealth, or anything to be remotely dignified by such a term, was first mooted, or rather it was a lively topic of debate long before Socialism was ever heard of. However, it did mount, and quite unavoidably, to a new point of intensity, once the world began to recognise the nature and accompaniments of the Soviet dictatorship.

Of course, the old pre-Soviet institutions sustained by force opposed and denounced the methods of force by which they in turn were overthrown and their interested exposures were discounted. Much more serious and persistent and devastating were the Socialist criticisms directed to the same end, for example, in the writings of George Orwell or Arthur Koestler, or, more subtly still, anticipating both of them, in the works of Ignazio Silone, who knew more about the actual subject than either.

"Every means tends to become an end," Silone had one of his characters write, and the physical and mental torture of both Italian Fascism and Soviet Communism were known to him as he wrote: "To understand the tragedy of human history it is necessary to grasp that fact. Machines which ought to be men's instrument, enslave him, the state enslaves society, the bureaucracy enslaves the state, the church enslaves religion, parliament enslaves democracy, institutions enslave justice, academies enslave art, the army enslaves the nation, the party enslaves the cause, the dictatorship of the proletariat enslaves Socialism. The choice and the control of the instruments of political action are thus at least as important as the choice of the ends themselves, and as time goes on the instruments must be expected to become an end for those who use them. Hence the saying that the end justifies the means is not only immoral; it is stupid. An inhuman means remains inhuman even if it is employed for the purpose of assuring human felicity. A lie is always a lie, murder is always murder. A lie always ends by enslaving those who use it, just as violence always enslaves those who use it as well as their victims."

Silone wrote those words in 1939; they make even sharper maxims in 1982, and let us not suppose that they apply only to the greatest questions of peace and war, of totalitarian victory or defeat in the contest for state power, they apply also to the lesser but still inescapable question about the means whereby Socialists should seek and carry through industrial change. Human beings and human communities cannot, by those who call themselves democratic Socialists, be viewed and used as guinea-pigs or ant-heaps, or, to use a more accurately horrifying metaphor, vivisected dogs. They must be moulded, consulted, and made the true masters of their fate.

For one thing, this means that the pace of industrial change must be suited to men and women, and not vice versa. The whole process of industrial change must itself be made subject to persuasion, to industrial democracy, to the democratic will of the communities involved.

I write as one who has witnessed and sought to guide the process of change in the great steel town of Ebbw Vale. It was once the foremost technically-proficient steel works in Britain or Western Europe, and its skilled steel makers retained that degree of proficiency long after industrial advance elsewhere had changed the prospect.

Whole neighbouring communities had been made dependent on steel: how could they ever imagine, how could some economists calculate, that so precious a commodity would lose its value? How could anyone guess that the settled prospects of the 1960s would be transformed by the 1980s, or that the whips of a steel recession would be followed by the scorpions of world slump? Or who can suppose that such uncontrolled lacerations can be an intelligent way to execute industrial advance, to enlarge the skills of the future, to entrench among our people a faith in democratic methods?

For some years in Ebbw Vale we did seek to execute such a planned transformation from one form of industry to another, albeit with imperfect weapons and powers and no majority in parliament. After May 1979, the exertion was cast aside and all in the interests of the godlike, dominant providential free market.

It will take a generation to repair the damage, and years more to establish what I believe should become a true, unbreakable Socialist objective to make the pace of change one which human beings and their communities can tolerate.

Or are we just content to let the juggernauts loose: to drive ruthlessly ahead to build the industrial equivalent of the skyscrapers which have been allowed to deface our cities: huge unwanted, monstrous emblems of how events may move too fast for people, for democracy.

I was taught this lesson by my wife, Jill, who has eyes to see with, a rare part of the anatomy not always possessed by Socialists, despite the longstanding example which they had all been set long since by one of the greatest of them, William Morris. Right from the first glimpse of those skyscrapers (and at the risk of a fierce quarrel with our friends on the Camden Council), she denounced those ghastly concrete ghettoes as an insult to the working-class. Would that I and others had heeded her better. William Morris, for sure, would have approved her bitter warnings.

And another of Marx's own contemporaries would have approved even more lustily. Alexander Herzen yielded to none in revolutionary fervour, but he would not abate for anyone, Marx included, his democratic allegiance. In his old age, some nihilist rivals from his Russian homeland told him to stop flagging his beloved stick-in-the-mud democracy. Herzen rebuked this "syphilis of revolutionary lusts", lamenting the ease with which his opponents despaired of everything, "the ferocious joy of their denial and their terrible ruthlessness. Despite their excellent spirits and noble intentions our bilious ones can, by their tone, drive an angel to blows and a saint to curses."

Indeed, he saw the fallacy in the Marxist method even while he recognised the glory of the Socialist ideal. He came to believe — as his most perceptive exponent has put it — "that remote ends were a dream, that faith in them was a fatal illusion; that to sacrifice the present, or the immediate and foreseeable future, to these distant ends must always lead to cruel and futile forms of human sacrifice" — a considerable prophecy for a democratic Socialist to make nearly 100 years before the Stalin show trials, the Stalin famines or the Polish Gethsemane of Christmas 1981.

To many (and to me), the Herzen doctrine may still appear too adamantly stated; some faith in those remote ends is required if the future is to be defined at all. But the Herzen doctrine certainly is required to rectify the moral balance between ends and means, to give the chance to breathe to those who must live from week to week, from day to day, to let them estimate for themselves what may be the nature and scale of the sacrifice.

Each generation, which can only live once, has the right to make its own choices. Socialists must insist on that principle no less resolutely than they seek to enlist enthusiasm for the creation of a new society. Of course, I am well aware that these cautionary admonitions and invocations, the whole caboodle together, will be cited as evidence of how my own Socialist convictions have become soft or mellow or something worse; how I have become shackled or suborned by events or pressures or, heaven help us, the corruption of power. Heaven help me, and my constituents and the labour movement!

It is the absence of power — the signs that the prospect might move from us — which enrages me. And if that tragic event were to occur — tragic for our party, tragic for our country — a part of the responsibility would rest with those who will not apply their minds to the enemy across our path, the next immediate battles; those who dismiss parliament as at best a mere platform; those who prefer the attractions of every sectarian side-turning, the new breed of Herzen's bilious ones; those who even dare contemplate the notion of postponing the exertion for electoral victory to the time after next. It is a measure of what injury our internal wrangling has done that such a treacherous notion should even dare to be hinted. But perspectives of this character on the so-called "hard" — an intellectual misnomer if ever there was one — left are not entirely novel.

William Hazlitt often directed his incomparable scorn against them. He wanted to return to the truly revolutionary questions of what could be and what should be done next. "Of all people", he insisted, "the most tormenting are those who by never caring about anything but their own sanguine, hair-brained Utopian schemes, have at no time any particular cause for embarrassment and despondency because they have never the least chance of success, and who by including whatever does not hit their idle fancy in the same sweeping clause of ban and anathema, do all they can to combine all parties in a common cause against them, and to prevent every one else from advancing one step farther in the career of practical improvement."

But against whom are these ancient invectives directed? Against Tony Benn and his associates? He could make the immediate retort that his own stock-in-trade was never of such an airy, philosophical, Utopian substance. Has he not concentrated his critical attack on immediate matters quite capable of resolution, such as the Labour Party's constitution, or the commonly accepted ideas about the deficiencies of parliamentary democracy? Has not Ignazio Silone himself, in the passage quoted above, delivered his own assault on the same target. He says: "Parliament enslaves democracy", and he had the good excuse of writing in the 1930s in an Italy where a pathetic imitation of a real parliament had opened the road to Fascism.

The Bennite accusations against our parliament or rather against the operation of the Parliamentary Labour Party, do not go so far, but they are central to the argument. They embrace a double accusation; first, the Parliamentary Labour Party over a period of years has allowed itself to become, thanks largely to Prime Ministerial and other forms of patronage, the plaything of the leader of the party, the obedient executor of the leadership in one form or another, while, second, the same Parliamentary Labour Party refuses to accept its proper subordinate position as the servant of the supreme Party Conference.

It was to remedy these deficiencies that the three constitutional changes were embarked upon and in some measure executed after the electoral defeat of May 1979 — the mandatory reselection of MPs, the establishment of an electoral college to elect the leader, and the proposal to remove the final control over the party manifesto from joint control of the party and the Parliamentary leadership where it is placed by the Constitution to the sole control of the Executive.

The two arguments have constantly been merged with each other in the public debate, thanks largely to Tony Benn's own presentation of the case, but they are in reality of a quite different calibre and significance, and the beginning of intelligence is to separate them properly.

So little is it true that Prime Ministerial or leadership patronage and influence have tightened their hold, that the history of the party in recent years might be much more faithfully described in exactly the opposite sense. The ineradicable fact is that compared with 15 or 20 years ago the power and independence of the individual Labour MP are vastly enhanced; he is much less at the beck and call of the whips and Party authority than ever he was.

Twenty and 30 years ago — at the height of the Bevanite disputes of the 1950s, for example — the fight of the Labour backbenchers, mostly leftwingers, was to establish their right to exercise their judgement and conscience as Socialist MPs against the detailed instructions of the party leadership in Parliament or the National Executive outside. Over the past two decades the practice — and the theory even — has been transformed. Partly the change was due to the deliberate relaxation of Party discipline introduced by the so-called Crossman-Silkin combination in the late 1960s; partly it was due to the experience of the 1974-79 Parliament when the precise registration of votes was more than ever required but when rigid discipline would never have secured it; partly it was due to the Labour Party coming of age as a Parliamentary Party.

After the May 1979 defeat, the new liberal method of working was reviewed by the Parliamentary Party itself, some improvements were examined and introduced, and the new liberal system was formally adopted by almost the entire Parliamentary Party in June 1981. Not much notice of this event was taken by the outside world then or thereafter; but the settlement reached then is unlikely to be upset and may have a significance greater than some other more sensationalised events.

Right, Left and Centre of the party gave their approval. Only a tiny handful demurred, and ironically its spokesmen came from the so-called hard-left minority. Their proposals for parliamentary operation would have re-instituted from a self-anointed left the rigid dictation of the party meeting which was once the chief instrument of the right. Fortunately for the future health of the party and parliament itself, the overwhelming majority of MPs remembered their history and applied its lessons.

Throughout the 80 years of the Labour Party's existence, the left within it has waged a consistent series of campaigns against what was condemned as the rigid application of the Standing Orders of the Parliamentary Party. It was this controversy of principle which led to the Independent Labour Party leaving the party in the 1930s, to some of the fiercest Bevanite rows of the 1950s, or to the infamous "dog licence" speech of Harold Wilson in the 1960s. Now with the declaration of June 1981 the old debate subsides. The charge that the Parliamentary Labour Party has in this field forfeited its rights to the leadership is the exact opposite of the truth.

No such conclusive verdict is conceivable or even desirable on the other major matter of contention concerning the respective authority of the Parliamentary Party and the Party Conference. Theoretically, the problem is insoluble; for the Constitution itself and, what is even more significant, the precedents applied over decades, have established two sovereign bodies, and neither will bow the knee to the other.

If the attempt is made to enforce such a final act of submission not merely the Constitution but the Labour Party itself would be disrupted. For it is inconceivable that the Party Conference would yield it legitimate policy-making powers to the party in parliament, and no less inconceivable that the Parliamentary Party would finally concede control over what it must do and pledge itself to do in parliament to a body outside. And it is inconceivable further that such a castrated body should still be potent enough to win a majority of British people in a free election.

As so often happens in constitutional arguments, at least in this country, a constitutional theory is found to possess a sound basis in common sense. No Party Conference, even if it contained the wisdom of a Solomon and the foresight of an Isaiah, can discern all the circumstances, and sometimes the most critical, in which a Labour Cabinet and a Parliamentary Party will have to act. To pretend so is just puerile. And, of course, it is a combination of such considerations which has preserved the balance over the years; for both the Party Conference and the parliamentary party have the supreme common enemy with their common strength mobilised for that purpose. Marxists should understand, even if Utopians may have other ideas.

However, the argument on those questions is rarely concerned with actual constitution-making, with the theoretical, or even the practical issues involved. Passions dig deeper, and the reason is that the issue is most frequently posed as a challenge to the good faith of the leaders involved and, by inference, of the bulk of the Parliamentary Party itself.

Were not the Labour Cabinets of the past — and most appositely the Labour Cabinet over which James Callaghan presided, from 1976 to 1979 — guilty of a deliberate and persistent abandonment of the Party Manifesto? Is not this the true cause of the rift between the leaders and the led, between the party inside parliament and the party outside? Is not this the reason why measures had to be taken by the rank and file, by the Party Conference, to bind the leaders and the Labour Party of the future?

The charge of bad faith or betrayal does, alas, figure quite prominently in the disputations of the left, as Tawney noted; it is one of the disagreeable aspects of the legacy left by Karl Marx. And, Marx or no Marx, Tawney or no Tawney, there is doubtless a psychological explanation why such excuses have an appeal. Anyhow the myth is widely accepted.

To answer the charge as it deserves would require a lengthy historical treatise, I content myself with a brief explosive outburst about why the application of the charge to the Callaghan Administration, of which I was a member, is a monstrous perversion. It is, first of all, somewhat galling to recall the first batch of measures which that Callaghan Administration set about carrying through, albeit with a majority of three or two or one or even less, which was all we had at our disposal. Five of those measures for a start had to be carried through on a guillotine motion, since there was no other way (moved, incidentally, by myself).

But they were all worth it. One brought the aircraft and shipbuilding industries into public ownership (where they still remain and where precious jobs are still retained, thanks to that Act passed in 1976); a second fulfilled a long-standing party commitment to abolish the tied cottage (and that Act still operates effectively too); a third Act provided the means of carrying comprehensive education much further (but much of that, alas, has been revoked); and the same reversal has been applied to the two other measures, one which abolished pay beds in hospitals and a second which extended industrial democracy on the docks. All those measures, be it noted, were Party Manifesto commitments, and all were carried out against more awkward parliamentary odds than any previous Labour Government had had to confront.

Time and again, throughout the period of the Callaghan Administration right from the beginning in April 1976 until the end of

May 1979 we (and by "we" I mean both the Cabinet and the Parliamentary Party, although clearly the responsibility rests most directly with the members of the Cabinet) were faced with painful choices. We never had the majority we would have wished to carry all we wanted, and we always had to calculate whether it was wise or expedient or defensible to stay in office securing so much less than we desired. Yet we also had to weigh in the balance what an incoming Tory government would mean for our people and whether that threat could be warded off temporarily and even permanently.

I always thought we had a chance to secure those objectives; I always thought we should work with all our strength to secure them. I always thought it would be defeatist and against the interests of Socialism itself, not to do everything in our power to that end, and meantime to carry through as much of the remaining parts of our Party Manifesto as we could. I thought any lesser effort — to have run away, to have thrown in our hands, to have opened the gates ourselves to a Thatcher government — would be, yes I repeat and underline the word, defeatist.

I thought that, and so, according to their actions, did the rest of the Cabinet and the overwhelming bulk of the party in parliament and out of it. Confronted with the choice at the time, this was always the verdict of all those concerned in the Cabinet itself. Now, years later, for all these vital tactical choices to be brushed aside as if they never existed — and for the accusation to be substituted that the Callaghan Cabinet was guilty of a great betrayal of the party and the manifesto — is to bowdlerise the historical process, to use no harsher term. And here it is pertinent to recall that when our attention was drawn, as I mentioned before, to the precedent of the MacDonald Cabinet, the answer was given on the spot, and not merely by words but by deeds.

The MacDonald Cabinet of 1931, facing a considerable economic crisis, proposed cuts in the livelihood of some of the poorest in the community, the unemployed, pensioners, the lowest paid. The Callaghan Cabinet, confronted with an economic crisis of at least equal proportions, sustained and improved the living standards of many of the poorest people in the country, the very groups now being hit by the Thatcher choices — the unemployed, the disabled, the pensioners, the lowest paid, those dependent on child benefit. That last was indeed a great reform, perhaps the greatest yet in the field of women's liberation, introduced at the very moment when the government faced the most severe economic test.

Those who do not trouble to note the difference are guilty of the crime against which Herzen inveighed so furiously. They seem ready to sacrifice one generation — and how many more? — to serve some distant goal, and they do not even stop to notice, as socialists should, that in this grisly process, it is the weakest who get hurt most. And if Socialist dialecticians fail to recognise that fact, the general public do not, they at least live in the present not in some theoretical and theatrical future.

But the times are too serious for all such reckonings and diversions. If the Labour Party were to lose the next parliamentary election, it would be the most fateful loss since the party was founded in 1900. More peremptorily than ever before, if in a new form, R H Tawney's fundamental question is presented to us: who is to be master? If democratic Socialists cannot secure the right answer at the next parliamentary opportunity, we may not be asked again, or rather this old famous Socialist stream could perish in sectarian bogs and sands.

If the Labour Party were to lose, to whatever combination of Tories, Liberals and Social Democrats, the first item on the agenda of two sections of the alliance, according to their own most pressing patriotic declarations, would be the introduction of a new electoral system designed to safeguard their own peculiar position for the future. It must be the first time in recent British history in which public men have come together on the basis of such a limited pre-eminent priority and recalls rather the spirit in which factions and sects might combine in the age of George III.

However the pronouncement must be taken seriously. One of the few public measures on which this same group of public men have found agreement in the past was in their readiness to transfer essential controlling power over the British economy from Westminster to Brussels. They would certainly not balk at the next step; to introduce some form of proportional representation both designed and equipped to ensure that all future British governments until the end of the century and beyond would take the character of some form of coalition. One road only would be barred: the road to democratic Socialism.

Such would be the result if the so-called Social-Democrats and their Liberal allies and their coalitionist hangers-on are allowed to make their much-heralded breakthrough at the next general election. Such seemed the direction in which the political scene was shifting at Warrington, Croydon and Crosby. Such has been the wretched news from many local government polls in recent months. Such could have been the calamitous result in a by-election at Bermondsey — and far beyond Bermondsey — if we had been compelled to fight on the declarations issued by the recently selected candidate there.

And those declarations, let me underline, did not assert the equality and inter-dependence of parliamentary and extra-parliamentary activities as the labour movement has practised them and the people of Britain understand and support them. Those declarations professed the superiority of extra-parliamentary activities as a means of securing change and progress in the Britain of the 1980s. They were anti-parliamentary and gave ruinous advantage and opportunities to our enemies — and to our Social Democrat enemies in particular.

Sooner or later, if the Labour Party was to prove afresh its allegiance to parliamentary democracy — and I mean the widely-held belief more than the actual institution — those declarations had to be repudiated. And, in my judgement as leader of the party, the sooner the better.

And here once again I am entitled to quote Tawney. He can bring us all back to reality: "Exponents of our brand of socialism must face the fact that, if the public, and particularly the working class public, is confronted with the choice between capitalist democracy, with all its nauseous insincerities, and undemocratic socialism, it will choose the former all the time. We must make it clear beyond the possibility of doubt that the Socialist Commonwealth which we preach will be built on democratic foundations."

Then he added, maybe with some premonition of our own disputes, that one "practical conclusion" involved in the acceptance of democracy as "the first premise of Socialism", was that "in the absence of an attempt to overthrow democracy, all nods, hints, winks and other innuendoes to the effect that violence is a card which Socialists keep up their sleeves, to be played when they think fit, are ruled out for good and all. All of them are fatuous, with the nauseous fatuity sometimes encountered during war in the ferocious babble of bellicose non-combatants."

For the men and women who made the Labour Party Constitution, and who insisted on seeking to establish a Labour Party inside parliament as well as outside in the country, were not mistaken. They understood the place parliament occupied in the history of the British people and the importance which our people attach to what Tawney called "the elementary decencies" of parliamentary government.

They understood that parliament was where disputes could be settled by consent instead of force. They understood that the left in politics, so much more than the right, with its traditional resort to actual fighting, had a vested interest in settling arguments peaceably. They understood maybe — William Lovett had an inkling of it — that what was achieved without resort to force would last much longer and better, that the Socialism won by such means might be the only kind worth having; that the words democratic Socialism should never be separated, that one was impossible without the other.

And those framers of the Constitution, as they wrote it in 1918, while the world was just emerging from what they dared to speak of as a war to end war, would have understood too the greater task still which awaits us, greater even than the constitution of the democratic Socialist state — the chance for Labour to help guide the nuclear weapon ridden world towards sanity and safety.

Democracy, direct action and socialism

Sean Matgamna

Margaret Thatcher and democracy

The cry "For Parliamentary Democracy: the Trotskyists are the enemy of democracy" is — perhaps predictably — the political standard under which Labour's right and soft left are trying to rally forces for a counter-offensive against the serious left.

The direct target is the revolutionary left. But the main target is the much bigger serious reformist left. The slippery Neil Kinnock has focused on this issue. The obvious intention is to confuse and divide the left which, when united, secured the victories of Brighton and Blackpool and which, if it can restore its unity, can still stop and beat back the present right-wing offensive.

Here, as when he sabotaged Tony Benn's campaign for deputy leader, Kinnock does the direct work of the right. Today, the Labour right has the union leaderships and the help of the media, but it is very weak among the rank and file of the Labour Party. Eighty-three per cent of the Labour Party's individual membership vote went to Benn for deputy leader. So the possibility of carrying through a purge of the Labour Party which will not gut it and immobilise it as an electoral force for years ahead depends on splitting the left.

The right want to isolate and drive out the Marxists, selectively purge the fighting reformist left, and intimidate the rest of the left. The attitude to democracy and parliament is the wedge which (they hope) will not only separate off the Marxists, but also inhibit and intimidate all those who want to struggle now against the Tory government in industry and on the streets.

Michael Foot could talk just one year ago of raising an extraparliamentary "storm of opposition to the government", and now some of the union leaders are talking — only talking — of industrial resistance to Tebbit's anti-union laws. But, says Michael Foot, there are limits. Parliament must rule — even on the bones of the labour movement. That is what the right wing want to say and what they want to get the labour movement to accept!

This Tory government acts towards many millions of its own people like an alien and hostile occupying power; and does not scruple to devastate British society and inflict poverty, unemployment, want and deprivation on our own people. But this government, in Michael Foot's view, has impeccable democratic credentials.

Foot, in histrionic mood, might well express his politics now by shouting across the floor of the House of Commons to Prime Minister Thatcher: "I disagree with everything you are doing, but I'll defend to the death your democratic right to do it!" Thatcher has a big majority in parliament, won in an election that was as fair and democratic as any election in Britain. But is the Thatcher government a democratic government?

Yes, according to the standards and norms of democracy in Britain (which is typical of bourgeois democracies). No, if by democracy is meant the best possible approximation to direct self-rule, or a system even minimally responsive to the interests of the electorate (and we are here talking, remember, about the most vital interests of whole communities and of an entire generation of young people). Thatcher does not have a mandate — and Michael Foot should not say that she has — to do what she has done to the youth, to whole industries and communities. Nobody voted for that: Thatcher would — to go by the polls and by-elections — have been dismissed within a year of election if the electorate had any mechanism by which to dismiss her. No mechanism exists.

It is 150 years since the British labour movement emblazoned on its banner the demand for annual parliaments. With annual parliaments what has happened in Britain in the last two years could have been stopped in June 1980. Yet those on the right of the labour movement who insist (I think rightly) that a socialist government should be willing to accept its own dismissal by a majority of the electorate are content that Thatcher should be free to play tyrant for five years.

Foot and his friends have forgotten the whole working class notion of developing and deepening the existing democratic structure. A strong case can be made out that Thatcher's government is the opposite of a democratic government — according to the conception of democracy it claims to base itself on.

One could, as we shall see, justify even armed insurrection against this government according to the principles of classical bourgeois democracy!

In the *Observer* of Sunday 10 January 1982, Michael Foot published the first part of his reply to the entire current of opinion among the rank and file of the Labour Party and trade unions which wants to challenge the Tories now, using extra-parliamentary direct action where necessary. He addresses those who reject, downgrade or are impatient with legalism and parliamentarism.

The mask of the Inquisition-master Torquemada raised like a visor above his face, Michael Foot mounts the rostrum of the *Observer* to preach a sermon on democracy to his loyal supporters, and to the heretics. It is more civilised than witch-burning: we will have to see whether it is instead of bonfires, or part of the preparation for them. Foot's basic ideas and his alternative to what he defines as Marxism deserve a reply.

Chapter 1: Is direct action against an elected capitalist government undemocratic?

The first thing that needs to be said about democracy is that they are lying about the Marxists and about our attitude to democracy. Those Liberals who "entered" the Labour Party long ago and made their careers as servants of the ruling class there, and those soft "lefts" like Kinnock who seem to believe in the divine right of the Liberals to rule the Labour Party, all lie through their teeth when they say that the revolutionary left is not concerned with democracy or is opposed to democracy, or will not defend democracy and fight for it.

The basic truth of the socialist labour movement and of unfalsified Marxism concerning the relationship of socialism to democracy, is this: whoever is not a democrat is not a socialist — nor a communist in the sense that Marx and Engels and Lenin and Trotsky understood the word and the goal. As long ago as 1848, Karl Marx and Frederick Engels wrote: "The first step in the revolution by the working class is to raise the proletariat to the position of ruling class, to win the battle of democracy." (*The Manifesto of the Communist Party*.)

Marxist socialists are democrats because we look to the working class and only to the working class to realise its own self-rule in socialism. The working class needs democracy for the same reason as it needs things like trade unions and political parties — because, unlike the bourgeoisie, it does not own major private property, and it can own the means of production and rule in society and in the state only collectively. It can know its own mind, assess its own experience, set its own goals and adjust them, and take care of all its own affairs, only collectively, and therefore only democratically.

This is true for the working class as a force fighting within capitalist society, and struggling to transcend it. It is true for the working class as the ruler of society, administering a planned economy.

Trotsky compared the function of democracy for the labour movement within capitalism and after it has overthrown it, to the function of oxygen for an animal. In both cases it is irreplaceable.

There are many qualifications (as we shall see) but that is the basic truth about democracy for socialists. When the right and the soft left say that the issue is "Parliamentary Democracy", they give it to be understood that the left are against democracy. They invoke the horrors of Stalinism against us as if this were the work of the left (who were the first victims of Stalinism!). They are engaging in a fraud.

For its effect, the right-wing's accusation depends on ignorance of what some socialists propose by way of reform of parliamentary democracy, or of what other socialists would replace it by — workers' councils. It depends on an absolute identification of "parliamentary democracy" with democratic rights, with liberty, and on the acceptance of parliament as the opposite of tyranny and totalitarianism and the only alternative to them. It depends on the acceptance of what now exists as "the best in the best possible of all democratic worlds". And they do that now with all the more edgy insistence because the reality the labour movement lives with in Britain is that parliament is being used to legitimate the naked class war directed at us by the Tory government.

It is a thoroughly dishonest exercise in intellectual card-sharping, dependent on the mental equivalent of sleight of hand. They define democracy in terms of only one of its historic forms, and try thereby to rule out of court those who would advocate either a different form of democracy or a more or less radical development of democracy on the basis of the existing parliamentary system.

In fact, the existing British system has had many different historical stages of growth and development. We have not known a steady perfecting of parliamentary democracy to an ideal present condition. On the contrary, the decline of the direct controlling power of the elected chamber, the House of Commons, has been going on for over 100 years In parallel to the extensions of the franchise after 1867, the ruling class has systematically created parallel levers of power, diminishing parliament. Real power has shifted from parliament to the cabinet, and then to the prime minister, backed by the unelected permanent bureaucracy.

The cry that parliamentary democracy is in danger is a truly ridiculous weapon to find in the hands of Labour parliamentarians who — like Michael Foot, for example — have for years and decades, in government and out, allowed themselves to function as so many mere parliamentary gargoyles, decorating and camouflaging the structure of unelected bureaucratic and military power which has grown to dominance within the facade of Britain's ancient parliamentary system.

Those who say we are the enemies of democracy have themselves surrendered many of the ancient rights of parliament to the civil service and the military. Many of them bear direct personal responsibility for the diminishing of parliamentary democracy, and for the consequent growth of political cynicism. And now they discover that parliamentary democracy is in danger — in danger from their critics and opponents in the labour movement!

Tony Benn has done tremendous work to bring to the attention of the labour movement the reality that now clothes itself in the traditional garb of the British parliamentary democratic system. He brings from his recent experiences as a government minister examples of the realities lurking behind the democratic facade, vindicating what revolutionary Marxists have said for many decades.

The permanent civil service to an enormous extent determines policy and ensures its continuity whatever government is in power: Benn once received a civil service brief marked, "For the new Minister, if not Mr Benn". Prime ministerial patronage ensures that parliament's role as a scrutineer of government is undercut and atrophied.

Real control of the armed forces — whose subordination to parliament at the end of the 17th century was the decisive final act in securing parliamentary rule in England — is therefore less and less exercised by parliament.

The former Chief of the General Staff, Lord Carver, has publicly admitted that in February 1974, when the last Labour government was returned amidst massive industrial struggles, senior army officers discussed "intervention"! In a debate with Pat Arrowsmith, Carver confirmed that the army officers had discussed a coup in February 1974. "Fairly senior officers were ill-advised enough to make suggestions that perhaps, if things got terribly bad, the army would have to do something about it." The top brass put a stop to it — but the top brass of the Chilean armed forces who were represented in Salvador Allende's cabinet didn't stop the fascistic coup of 1973 which pulverised the Chilean labour movement. They organised it.

In Britain the "fairly senior officers" of 1974 are now probably "senior" or close to it. Five months before the events Lord Carver referred to, the *Times* had commented on the Chile coup in this alarming fashion: "Whether or not the armed forces were right to do what they have done, the circumstances were such that a reasonable military man could in good faith have thought it his constitutional duty to intervene." (*Times*, 13 September 1973).

Tony Benn, 11 years a member of Labour governments in the 60s and 70s, governments supposedly in control of Britain, has recently summed up the state of British democracy. These are some of his conclusions:

"Despite all that is said about democracy and our traditional freedoms, the people of Britain have much less control over their destiny than they are led to believe... and a great deal less than they had a generation ago. In short, the powers which control our lives and our futures have become progressively more concentrated, more centralised, more internationalised, more secretive and less accountable. The democracy of which we boast is becoming a decorous facade behind which those who have power exercise it for their own advantage and to the detriment of the public welfare."

Benn is especially concerned with the loss of British autonomy to the IMF and the EU. But the following has nothing directly to do with Britain's position in the world:

"A hereditary House of Lords, topped up by the pliable recipients of prime ministerial patronage, still has great power to delay or obstruct the policies adopted by an elected House of Commons. It also has an unfettered veto, in law, to protect itself from abolition. The Crown still retains an unfettered legal authority to dismiss an elected government, dissolve an elected House of Commons, and precipitate a general election at any time it chooses. To do so it need only call upon its prerogative powers as used by the Governor General of Australia when the Labour government of Gough Whitlam was dismissed... All cabinet ministers derive their executive authority, in its legal sense, not from election as leaders of the majority party in the Commons, but as members of Her Majesty's Government, formed by the prime minister at the Crown's invitation... But the courts and the armed forces swear allegiance to the Crown and not to the elected government."

Though Benn's writings are of great value in opening the eyes of the broad labour movement to the realities behind the parliamentary facade, none of this is very startling to Marxists. For example, Trotsky wrote this in *Where is Britain Going?* in 1925:

"'The royal power', declare the Labour Party leaders, 'does not interfere' with the country's progress... The royal power is weak because the instrument of bourgeois rule is the bourgeois parliament, and because the bourgeoisie does not need any special activities outside of parliament. But in case of need, the bourgeoisie will make use of the royal power as a concentration of all non-parliamentary, i.e. real forces, aimed against the working class."

Tony Benn asks what would happen "if a government elected by a clear majority on a mandate of reform were to introduce legislation to complete the process of democratic advance". This: "The Lords veto, the prerogative of the crown to dismiss and dissolve, and the loyalties of the courts and the services to adjudicate upon legitimacy and to enforce those judgements might all be used to defend the status quo against a parliamentary majority elected to transform it."

Writing not long before Denning ruled the electors of London incompetent to vote for the higher rates and cheap public transport policy on which the Labour majority on the GLC campaigned and won the election, Benn felt obliged to add: "This may seem far-fetched, but at least these forces opposed to democratic reforms could argue that they were operating in accordance with the letter of the constitution, even though in no sense with its spirit... The British constitution reserves all its ultimate safeguards for the non-elected elite.

"The democratic rights of the people can, in a crisis, be adjudicated to be illegal, thus legitimising the military in extinguishing them" (from 'Britain as a Colony', in *Arguments for Democracy*, 1981).

It is the measure of the soft left, like Michael Foot and Neil Kinnock, though no more than you would expect from the Labour right, that just at this point they discover that it is the serious left which threatens the future of parliamentary democracy in Britain!

It is the ruling class who threaten the democracy we have now. Under the influence of profound social crisis, the British political system will begin to display its undemocratic side as, and to the degree that, the ruling class begins to have need for extra democratic safeguards.

Read what Ian Gilmour, a former chair of the Tory party, says: "Conservatives do not worship democracy. For them majority rule is a device... Majorities do not always see where their best interests lie and then act upon that understanding. For Conservatives, therefore, democracy is a means to an end, not an end in itself.

"In Dr Hayek's words, democracy 'is not an ultimate or absolute value and must be judged by what it will achieve'. And if it is leading to an end that is undesirable or inconsistent with itself, then there is a theoretical case for ending it. 'Numbers in a state', said Burke, 'are always of consideration, but they are not the whole consideration'. In practice no alternative to majority rule exists, though it has to be used in conjunction with other devices."

Listen to the brutal truth expressed by Bonar Law, Tory Irish Home Rule leader during threatened Tory revolt against a Liberal government (and later briefly a prime minister): "There are things stronger than parliamentary majorities".

IS DIRECT ACTION AGAINST AN ELECTED CAPITALIST GOVERNMENT UNDEMOCRATIC?

On the eve of World War One, sections of the British ruling class and the army, and the entire Tory party, raised a storm of revolt against the Liberal government's decision to give Ireland Home Rule. There was an officers' revolt in the British army in Ireland. They armed and drilled a large — orange — private army (armed with German guns). They succeeded. They forced the Liberal government to abandon its plan to solve Ireland's British problem by way of an all-Ireland Home Rule parliament. Eventually, partition and all that has flowed from it came as a result of this Tory revolt.

Under the pressure of the social crisis, British parliamentary democracy can and probably will enter a downward spiral of decline — especially when the working class and the labour movement begin to recover from the effects of the slump and start to fight back.

The reckless distortion and savage misrepresentation of the left by the establishment media which is poisoning the political climate in Britain now, that is itself a small token of how willing the ruling class is to use the big stick when necessary.

A "democratically" entrenched Tory government is now legally devastating the working class and constitutionally trying to beat down the labour movement. The issue is whether to fight the Tories or let them destroy much of what the labour movement has won.

When the Parliamentary Labour Party denies the labour movement's right to fight back against the Tories in the name of the divine right of parliament and when, against the labour movement, the PLP claims for itself the status, respect and prerogatives of the once-sovereign parliament of the UK, then what was said of another historical parody can justly be said of them.

The PLP is turning into the ghost of British parliamentary democracy. It is attempting to crown itself irremovable sovereign lord of the labour movement, perched atop the near-ruins of the decrepit parliamentary system — a system which it can neither replace, regenerate, reform nor (if it comes to it) defend against the assault of the ruling class.

Chapter 2: The appeal to history

Foot invokes the saints of British radicalism (even the suffragettes — who were, technically, small-scale terrorists and mostly not at all radical except on votes for women). He justifies their extraparliamentary actions and claims their tradition for himself. But today it is different, he says — because then, either parliament was not available to the people at all, or the radicals were fighting for a sectional interest shut out from parliament's all-transforming portals.

Wat Tyler (who led the Peasants' Revolt 600 years ago) "had no representative to whom he could put his case". Did Oliver Cromwell knock parliament about a bit? By Cromwell parliament was "first saved... and then shut down when it proved obstreperous". Foot considers that there were good democratic grounds for Cromwell's action because "the men of Cromwell's armies... did represent a much larger total of the British people of their century than the parliament" which Cromwell shut down. So Foot can set it all to democratic rights in his head by an arithmetical computation three and a quarter centuries later; and Cromwell was a good democrat even against parliament!

As to the first mass workers' party, the Chartists of the 1830s and 40s: "Their declared aim was to establish a parliament which they could trust, not one they wished to bypass. Extra-parliamentary action was important since they had no voice inside; actually to win the voice inside was the aim." So Foot approves of their extra-parliamentary activities too.

In fact, the Chartists wanted a lot more than a voice. They wanted power to subordinate society to their own interests. Then the vote was power, parliament really did have the power; that is why the ruling class would have had civil war rather than working class suffrage. If the Chartists' formal demands now seem moderate, it is because something seemingly like some of them has been realised — without the radical purpose the Chartists pursued by way of these demands being realised. But in their time the Chartists were like the "moderates" in James Connolly's song — "We only want the earth".

Foot is wrong — factually and politically — to imply that the Chartists won all of even the formal goals for which "they were right" to fight outside parliament. They demanded annual parliaments. Where would Mrs Thatcher be now if that elementary precondition of a healthy democracy had been won then? Logically, if he thinks the Chartists were right to fight for annual parliaments, Foot should favour struggle now to bring down the Tory government!

The suffragettes wrecked property, attacked parliament, raised fires and planted small bombs. But Foot argues that they were justified "precisely because they too were denied the right to speak and act inside parliament." "It is an irony," says Foot, "that they should now be paraded as the opponents of parliamentary methods." But surely not as big an irony as that they should be presented — because their aim was to get the parliamentary vote — as exponents of parliamentary methods!

In fact they were characterised above all by rejection of parliamentary methods: they hived off from the numerous mere suffragists who favoured parliamentary methods, and from a large lobby of MPs which fought for women's suffrage year in and year out around Private Members' Bills. Far from "lacking a voice" in parliament, in fact they got a majority in the House of Commons at least once, only to see it vetoed by the House of Lords. But that veto had been curbed by the time of the wildest suffragette activities. Still, Foot says, it was permissible to the suffragettes to act as they did from impatience with parliament, and, before 1911, because of frustration with the House of Lords' entrenched power.

Then what about the working class now? Thatcher's Tories are destroying jobs and communities; they will not be restored quickly, if ever. The trade unions are being put in a legal straitjacket. Why do we not have the same right of impatience with parliament and the parliamentary processes? Why, in addition, do we not have the right of extra-parliamentary activity for self-defence? After the ruling against London Transport, do we not have as good grounds for impatience with the House of Lords as the suffragettes did? If and when the undemocratic legal reserve powers of the British state are used, why should we not treat legality as the suffragettes (with Foot's approval) did? There is no reason why we should not. Foot's invocation of the now safe (because past) causes celebres of his radical tradition implies, justifies and recommends not his politics, but ours.

Of all his historical examples, Foot says, in effect: "Of course, to achieve such results [a voice in parliament] it was necessary to take action outside parliament, and with every justice". The message is necessarily that those were bad days, and now we have a perfect democratic machine (even if not quite what the Chartists fought for). But this is simply not true: the depredations of the minority Thatcher government are the glaring, painful proof of it! When Michael Foot talked last year of raising a storm of protest against the government, and led a great march through

Liverpool, he was rather feebly carrying on the real traditions of those struggles; when he cants against extra-parliamentary action he is betraying them. He invokes limited, ancient, and now respectable radical causes, all the better to attack those who actually stand now in the living continuity of those causes. Foot invokes all these old radical causes, but in fact his attitude to parliament now resembles nothing so strongly as the attitude of the Anglican Tories in the reign of James II! Committed to the idea of the divine right of kings and the sinfulness of resistance to a legitimate king, they confronted the Catholic king's machinations to destroy their church and restore Catholicism. They found it impossible to agree with James, naturally, but also impossible to resist him; to resist would have been a very great sin. Their policy, too, might have been shouted across the House of Lords by some purple-clad ancestor of Foot's: "I disagree bitterly with what you are doing, but I'll defend to the death your right to do it!" When others kicked James off the throne and made the "Glorious Revolution" in 1688, these people still stood by King James and his divine Stuart right to rule! Passively, it is true: they would not do anything for James. But they never did anything against him. Consistent in their boneheaded dogmatism, they retained their sterile loyalty to James even when he was gone, and faced persecution, in the fashion of those days, at the hands of James' conquerors.

They, Michael Foot — useless alike to James and his enemies — are your political ancestors; Cromwell and the others you claim as your own are really ours! They believed in the people's right of resistance to tyrants, social, political or religious; they were fighters, not canting priests paralysed by superstition and a doctrine that the entrenched powers had a divine right even to be tyrannical.

For Foot now it is not the divine right of kings but the divine right of parliament and the compelling legitimacy it confers even on a naked class war government like Thatcher's. Foot is ambitious: he wants to decorate the right-wing Labour float in the democratic carnival with the heads of Marx, Engels and Trotsky. Marx and Engels envisaged, says Foot, that in England there might be a peaceful transition to socialism. He quotes Engels (selectively) to this effect. This is less than serious. Marx and Engels did talk about the possibility of peaceful socialist transformation in Britain, the USA and perhaps (Marx said he didn't know enough about its institutions to be sure) Holland. Why? Because in those states the bureaucratic/military system was not a major force. And is that still true in Britain today? Read Tony Benn's account of the realities of rule in

Britain today!

Trotsky and Lenin, says Foot, only "thought perhaps that other parliaments might be as futile or obstructive for their purposes as the Russian Duma". They made the mistake of thinking the British parliament was "fashioned in the same mould" as the Duma! This assertion means only that Foot has not read or has forgotten, Trotsky's detailed analysis of British politics, *Where is Britain Going?*

Trotsky, says Foot, "would never have been guilty of the infantile, querulous condemnations of parliament and parliamentary action which some of his self-styled followers adopt... Trotsky, the foremost literary genius brought forth by the Soviet Revolution, would surely have disowned with one sweep of his pen the whole breed of modern Trotskyists" (because of our sins of literary style?). It is quite true that some of those calling themselves Trotskyists have many of the traits of anarchism, and sometimes come close to rejecting parliamentary action. The attitude of the Socialist Workers' Party (SWP) to the Labour Party, for example, is a necessary by-product of its attitude to parliamentary action — one of dismissal, and the pretence that it is irrelevant. (But in fact they do believe in democracy — workers' democracy, through workers' councils).

Effectively the SWP rejects political action — except for general socialist propaganda, work to "build the party", and promises of what they may do sometime in the future, counterposed to the realities of the labour movement now. Marx polemicised against the sort of "political indifferentism" the SWP represents when he encountered it in its brave and open early anarchist form. So did Trotsky. But there aren't any SWP-ers in the Labour Party!

Foot is trying to tar Labour Party activists with this brush, not because they share the SWP's anti-political traits, but on the contrary because, unlike the SWP, they are politically active within the broad labour movement, and have shaken up its political etc. structures. He drags this in to cover his own tracks, and as a means to separate himself from the present-day radicals and revolutionaries whose traditions he invokes, tries to appropriate, and seems to genuinely respect.

He concedes that "it is not possible or desirable that the socialist acceptance of parliamentary institutions should be automatic or uncritical or unqualified". But Foot himself does accept these institutions without other than historical qualification, and accepts confinement to them not just automatically but by deep reflex and ingrained dogmatic conviction.

Here Foot's radical conscience pays historical tribute to his current vices: "the Labour Party needs to use parliament more ambitiously and more deliberately than ever before". Yes! Even the quasi-syndicalists of the SWP would agree with that. So why does Labour Party leader Foot continue to collaborate with Thatcher? Why not take up Tony Benn's call for "disengagement", i.e. boycott of the Tory structures? That would not be enough, but it would be something. But in fact Foot raised this idea because he needs to have an apparent alternative to offer to the indicated use of trade union power now to stop Thatcher: "the dominant need is to turn the nation's mind to parliamentary action". He insists that "trade union power cannot save us, particularly since at such a perilous time the trade unions are compelled to conduct defensive, rearguard battles."

Trade unions as trade unions cannot offer an overall framework for socialist transformation, unless they become a great deal more than trade unions. But they can resist, fight back, make it impossible for the government to govern. They could even bring down the government. What does Foot think of the events in 1972 — one of the great, historic victories of the labour movement — when a wave of spontaneous political strikes forced the TUC to call a one-day general strike for a political purpose and, before the strike date set, forced the government to release the five dockers who had quite legally been jailed according to an Act of Parliament democratically passed, stamped and signed in accordance with the best of all possible parliamentary democratic constitutions? A petition to parliament should have been organised? Good democrats, socialists as well as others, should have denounced the workers whose actions forced open the gates of Pentonville jail for the five dockers? Direct action against the democratically elected government's democratically decided law released those dockers: the lack of direct action (partly because people relied on the Labour government) was probably decisive in keeping the three Shrewsbury building pickets in jail (in Des Warren's case, for three years).

Why does the once socialist Michael Foot need this rigmarole? Because he is afraid of the alternative — all-out struggle against Thatcher. He knows that Britain's democracy is skin deep. He knows what might have happened in Britain in the mid-70s, when army officers plotted a military coup. His Observer articles sent a message to such people that the Labour leaders could do the job for them, bloodlessly.

Jack Jones, Michael Foot's trade union alter ego during the last Labour government — 1974-1979, has publicly explained the right turn of the trade union leaders and the government in July 1975 in terms of the terrible dangers facing Britain — including the danger of a military coup.

Michael Foot knows that the danger of the ruling class using its reserve powers or the armed forces, or both, against a properly elected democratic government is a very real one when they feel threatened. His solution to this problem is to say: don't threaten them!

Rhetorically, he offers the following advice to "those self-styled revolutionaries who speak today too readily of the resort to illegal methods or to street battles"; "those who think socialism is to be won there should at least train to become soldiers or policemen — to face the stormtroopers". And what if the coming of the storm-troopers does not flow from working class direct action on the streets, but from a left wing victory in a general election? What if the storm-troopers are likely to be sent as the result of a radical electoral victory like that of Salvador Allende in Chile, who was overthrown and murdered by the army in September 1973? Perhaps the same conclusion would follow, and not only rhetorically.

Serious socialists who try to function as the memory of the working class, learning from history, have long known that these conclusions do follow. A serious working class leader, faced with the facts of history and with the personal experience of the British armed forces' reaction to labour militancy and the election of a Labour government in 1974, would reach Foot's conclusion above not rhetorically but in deadly earnest. He or she would campaign for the disbandment of the armed forces and the creation of a workers' militia.

But, like all the right and the soft left, Foot prefers to lie to himself and to the labour movement about the present condition of British democracy. Why? Because Foot is mesmerised by the democratic forms and facades of parliamentary democracy. He forgets that democracy is democracy only if it allows the people to actually govern themselves in their own interests. So mesmerised that he seems not to notice that we do not have such a democratic system. So mesmerised that, even though he knows that if the working class were to try to use parliament against the interests of the ruling class then the "storm-troopers" would be unleashed, all he can do with that knowledge is turn it into rhetoric against working class action now, trying to convince us of his own belief that democracy is most secure when the ruling class and its storm-troopers are armed to the teeth, and the labour movement disarmed.

This is the crux of it: for Foot, radical direct action is now superseded by parliament. The labour movement must bow down to parliament. A government which can command a parliamentary majority may do anything it likes to the labour movement — and Foot will be the first to shout his denunciations at those who resist and tell the labour movement it should rebel; and that in reality it will be acting when it rebels according to the great traditions of British radicalism, which created our now half-moribund democratic parliamentary system.

With this attitude Foot betrays even the pre-socialist radical tradition which he does — as far as I can judge — sincerely revere. The great bourgeois revolutions, born of struggle against oppressive systems and tyrants, wrote into their constitutions the right of revolt. The American Declaration of Independence of 1776, for example, states: "We hold these truths to be self-evident, that all men are created equal: that they are endowed by their Creator with certain unalienable rights; that among these are life, liberty and the pursuit of happiness.

"That, to secure these rights, governments are instituted among men, deriving their just powers from the consent of the governed; that, whenever any form of government becomes destructive of these ends, it is the right of the people to alter or abolish it, and to institute a new government, laying its foundation on such principles, and organising its powers in such form as to them shall seem most likely to effect their safety and happiness... When a long train of abuses and usurpations, pursuing invariably the same object, evinces a design to reduce them under absolute despotism, it is their right, it is their duty, to throw off such government and to provide new guards for their future security".

According to this, it could be argued that it is such sustained tyranny and oppression for Thatcher to do what is being done now — and cannot be undone easily — that it justifies even an armed revolt against the Tory government! The labour movement has every right to struggle outside of parliament against this government — according to the idea of democracy in which in the last analysis parliament has power and authority. If the constitution does not oblige Thatcher to let the electorate throw her out, why should the electorate be bound by such a manifestly inadequate constitution? Why should the labour movement listen to Foot telling us that we must submit and that it is a crime against democracy to resist?

The classical bourgeois theory of parliamentary democracy not only recognised this right of resistance, but proclaimed it as itself one of the basic principles of democratic government. The truth is that the Labour right and Foot do not stand for either the spirit or letter of parliamentary democracy as understood by those like the American revolutionaries; for them it was a real, practical, living set of principles to govern the behaviour of their class in its time of vigour and progress.

By parliamentary democracy Foot and his friends mean the shell and the forms. Theirs is the conservative and timid constitutionalism that would have sustained the status quo of Charles I, the unreformed parliament before 1832, or the exclusively middle class House of Commons before 1867, which excluded the mass of men and women from the suffrage.

It happens that theirs is the constitutionalism of a formally advanced bourgeois democracy. Their political ancestors did not win it: ours did! They do not stand in the true line of those who cranked that parliamentary democracy forward by way of revolution (the 1640s, 1688-9) and successive reforms. They counterpose the partly ossified, reshaped and neutralised, and now inadequate, results of past revolutions and mass struggles to the present living labour movement with its needs and struggles — the struggles to deepen democracy, to defend the labour movement: the struggle for a different, socialist system. Michael Foot and all his political brothers and sisters worship not the once-radiant face of bourgeois democracy, but its historic backside. Its face belongs to us.

Chapter 3: The scarecrow of Stalinism

In part 2 of his written oration on parliamentary democracy and those whom he denounces as its enemies (*Observer*, January 17 1982), Michael Foot attempts to answer the challenge he had posed to himself in part one.

There, he ended by promising to undertake the difficult task of replying to those whose rejection of the idea that there can be a peaceful parliamentary road to socialism in Britain was expressed in R H Tawney's brilliant image which Foot quoted thus: "Onions can be eaten leaf by leaf, but you cannot skin a live tiger paw by paw... If the Labour Party is to tackle its job with some hope of success, it must mobilise behind it a body of conviction as resolute and informed as the opposition in front of it."

Foot commented: "In other words, Tawney recognised the existence of the class struggle and the mighty convulsions required to secure its exorcism." But nobody with even a slight awareness of the facts of history or of present-day Britain would now deny the existence of the class struggle!

Even Ramsey McDonald, the right-wing Labour prime minister, and the renegade who went over to the Tories and became their captive figurehead prime minister in the anti-working class "National Government" in 1931, recognised the class struggle. He used to boast that while of course he recognised the class struggle, he — unlike the revolutionaries — deplored it and regarded it as something to be moved away from, abandoned, outgrown, patched up; it was not something the left should fight as if they meant to win it.

Serious socialists regard the class struggle as something to be fought in a spirit that takes account of the realities of class society and the facts of history. It will only be exorcised after it has been won by the working class, after the spectre of socialism has become solid social fact. A thousand terrible victories by the ruling classes will not exorcise it, because they cannot abolish class society: only the working class can do that. The idea that the class struggle can "be exorcised" by the labour movement agreeing to limit itself, by a historic self-denying ordinance, to certain methods of struggle, is an absurd idea that directly serves the ruling-class side in the unavoidable struggle. The class struggle is ineradicable and it will last as long as class society lasts. The idea that, in the interests of "democracy", the workers should not seriously fight the class struggle is an ideological weapon of the ruling class to help tie the hands of its working class opponents. The bourgeoisie fights the class struggle all the time!

He may not know it, but Foot's article is a weapon of the bourgeoisie fighting the battle of ideas inside the labour movement. What is distinctive about Tawney's image is not the bare recognition of the fact of class struggle, but the rejection of the possibility that it can be resolved peacefully, that the ruling class will peacefully allow itself to be divested of its wealth or of the power to defend that wealth. The ruling class does indeed have tiger's claws, and it will use them when it needs to. The ruling class is "armed to the teeth", and, as Foot in passing recognises in part one, it does dispose of storm troopers.

It is the measure of Michael Foot's politics now that he finds Tawney's comment noteworthy for its mere recognition of the fact of class struggle, and that, astonishingly, he so misreads Tawney as to think that is the point he is making. In fact, Foot never actually gets round to directly discussing, still less refuting, the point that makes Tawney's image arresting and central to the dispute between reformists and revolutionaries: however peaceful and legal we are, the ruling class will not let us win socialism peacefully, and we can only get our heads clawed off if we approach the matter with naive trust in the myths of parliamentary democracy.

As an advertisement for part 2, Foot in part 1 had said: "After all we should have learned something from half a century [since Tawney] of such tumult and terror in human affairs. And part of what we have learnt, or should have learnt, adds up to a direct refutation of apocalyptic Marxism, or, if you wish, a justification, in quite a different sense from the old one, of [the Fabian slogan of] the inevitability of gradualness. Throughout those years, several different rivers of experience merge into the same torrent", which he promised to "explore".

In fact the gist of his reply in part 2 is that he rejects the idea of socialism as something radically different from capitalism. He does not argue that in fact you can skin the tiger paw by paw. We can, he implies, escape the tiger's violence if we give up all thought of skinning it! It is the goal of socialism Foot thereby rejects, not "apocalyptic Marxism" as he says. For Foot now, there is to be no socialist transformation, no socialism as something distinct from capitalism — only civilised, decent Labour government, concerned with ameliorations and reforms while helping the bourgeoisie run capitalism. And the goal of returning and then sustaining such a Labour government now displaces all other goals.

His discussion of peaceful or non-peaceful roads to socialism is thus purely academic, because, essentially, he resolves the dilemma he has posed for himself, quoting Tawney, by abandoning the goal of socialist transformation. And in fact there is only one stream to Michael Foot's "torrent", and that is the experience of Stalinist totalitarianism. In the nature of things, Foot can not examine the other great mid-20th century stream of working class experience, that of the supine reformists whose weaknesses helped generate both Stalinism and fascism.

His way of "replying" to what Tawney said about the tiger is to quote Tawney 20 years later, in the 1950s, writing thus: "The truth is that a conception of socialism which views it as power, on which all else depends, is not, to speak with moderation, according to light. The question is not merely whether the state owns and controls the means of production. It is also who owns and controls the state. It is not certain, though it is probable, that socialism can in England be achieved by the methods proper to democracy. It is certain that it cannot be achieved by any other."

Foot adds emphasis to the last sentence. Tawney and his politics is a subject in itself. The use Foot makes of him is astonishing! According to Foot, when Tawney invoked the tiger which will not voluntarily be skinned, he was writing "before he and most others had examined the full nature of Soviet totalitarianism". And somehow the fact of Stalinist totalitarianism qualifies that — essentially irrefutable — image of the tiger who will not be skinned peacefully and renders it obsolete. Only if the goal of skinning the capitalist tiger is abandoned — because of Stalinism! — does Tawney's image become obsolete! Tawney uses the general term "by the methods of democracy" where Foot gives it the most narrow reading to mean "exclusively by the methods of parliamentary legality".

Foot presumes Tawney meant "peaceful methods" (though whether only peaceful methods are democratic is in fact open to argument, as we have seen). But in any case Tawney (as quoted) argued only that such methods would probably be sufficient, not that they would certainly be so. He left the alternative open, where Foot closes it completely, thereby disavowing in advance the right of the labour movement to self-defence against the organs of state repression, which in Foot's best of all possible democracies remain in the hands exclusively of the ruling class. And importantly the right of the labour movement to skin the capitalist tiger.

The question Tawney poses: "who owns the state?" is indeed at the heart of socialism. It defines the difference between socialism and state collectivism. Foot's implication that mass democratic action outside parliament would somehow place the state outside the control of the people is, truly, bizarre. Bizarre, too, is Foot's use of Tawney's reflections on

Stalinism — the untrammelled power of the totalitarian state bureaucracy over all of society including the working class — to justify his policy of leaving all power in the hands of the bourgeoisie, and its "stormtroopers", and not daring to fight to resist Thatcher's government for fear of them.

Foot does three impermissible things here. First, he equates Stalinism with a form of socialism, accepting the preposterous self-justification of the Stalinist ruling class as a force embodying and struggling for a form of socialism. Unfortunately its methods are bad (Foot argues) and destroy a (presumably) acceptable socialist end.

Foot links and identifies the totalitarian system that has now existed in the USSR for over 50 years (and which has been replicated in many other countries) with the workers' revolution of 1917. He locates the root of totalitarianism in the Original Sin committed in 1917 by the Russian workers when they used violence to take power. Thus he equates any violence by the labour movement — implicitly even defensive violence — with the germ of totalitarianism. Thus only "the methods of democracy", by sleight of hand identified as those of the decrepit British parliamentary system now (even including its blatantly undemocratic secondary rules) are permissible.

The third impermissible step in Foot's polemic is the pretence that his references to Stalinism have anything to do with what he is in dispute with the serious Labour Party left about now. No, they do not!

By "the methods proper to democracy" or by totalitarian methods, meaning working-class direct-action methods: that is Foot's way of posing the alternatives. But it is ahistorical, illogical, and for the immediate issue beside the point. The issue which remains to be argued is whether the "methods proper to democracy" should or can exclude extra-parliamentary actions to stop the Tories now, or violent self-defence against ruling-class violence, or violent revolutionary action by a working class majority to deprive the ruling class and its state of the means of threatening or using violence against the labour movement. They are the issue. Stalinist totalitarianism is something else again.

The argument about ends and means, says Foot truly, "did mount to a new point of intensity, once the world began to recognise the nature and accompaniments of the Soviet dictatorship".

Those overthrown in the Russian Revolution had denounced the force used to overthrow them, records Foot. "Much more serious and persistent and devastating were the socialist criticisms directed to the same end —

George Orwell, Arthur Koestler, and Ignazio Silone." With this self-chosen political genealogy, Foot firmly places himself in the ranks of those who in the 30s and 40s abandoned socialism for, at best, liberal reformism, in response to the degeneration of the Russian Revolution.

"Every means tends to become an end", he quotes the one-time pre-Stalinist communist Silone. "Machines which ought to be man's instruments enslave him, the state enslaves society, the bureaucracy enslaves the state, the church enslaves religion, parliament enslaves democracy, institutions enslave justice, academics enslave art, the army enslaves the nation, the party enslaves the cause, the dictatorship of the proletariat enslaves socialism".

"Parliament enslaves democracy", would serve well as an epitaph for Foot himself. For the rest, Silone is talking about Stalinism. As a communist of the heroic period who broke with the Communist International in 1929, as it was becoming something qualitatively different from the revolutionary organisation set up by Lenin and Trotsky, Silone knew something about the differences between Stalinism and Bolshevism.

What is centrally wrong with all Foot's arguments here is indeed the identification of Stalinism and Bolshevism. Foot insists on the ridiculous and false identification of the workers' revolution of 1917 with the totalitarian dictatorship of the bureaucracy over the working class which was established in a bloody civil war against the workers and peasants of the USSR after 1928 (a civil war in which only one side, the bureaucracy, was armed and organised). Bolshevism in 1917 was a political tradition in the Russian labour movement which concentrated in itself the self-liberating energy of the revolutionary workers, and led them to take and consolidate state power in most of the former Tsar's empire.

The Russian workers armed themselves, and used force to disarm or destroy those who were in arms against them. They were organised in a democratic network of workers' councils elected in factories and districts and linked together across Russia. Elections were frequent and delegates were easily recallable. It was a far more flexible representative, responsive system, controllable by the masses, than any parliament such as the existing British one can ever be.

This system was intended to do without permanent state bureaucrats (and for a while it succeeded). The armed forces which made the revolution were the Red Guard — a workers' militia, which was essentially more or less identical with formations like the flying picket squads of miners, builders or steel workers which we have known in Britain over the last decade — except that they were armed, that they disarmed the bourgeoisie and its agents and supporters, and that they themselves became the state power.

That was the Russian workers' revolution. 65 years later, it is a proper subject for critical minded socialists whether everything done by the armed workers and by the workers' party led by Lenin and Trotsky was well done, and whether anything they did contributed to the rise of Stalin later on. But to identify the 1917 revolution with Stalinism is preposterous!

It was the opposite of totalitarianism: mass, armed working class (and initially peasant) democracy. They would rightly have replied in Trotsky's words to the notion that "methods proper to democracy" meant excluding armed self-defence or offensive action against the armed forces of the ruling class: "The reformists systematically implant in the minds of the workers the notion that the sacredness of democracy is best guaranteed when the bourgeoisie is armed to the teeth and the workers are unarmed. "

Not only were they the opposite of totalitarianism, in the sense given to the word by Stalin, Mussolini, and Hitler, they were in the existing conditions of Russia in 1917 and after the only alternative to bloody ruling-class dictatorship. If the vacillating middle of the road government of Kerensky had not given way to the workers' power it would have given way to the armed reaction, based on sections of the army. The pioneering fascist-style counter-revolutionary movement would have emerged in Russia, not, as happened (when the Italian workers failed in 1919-20 to take power) in Italy.

Foot says that Stalinist "apologists have never been able to explain how the enormities of Stalinism happened — or what guarantee there can be that they should never develop again."

No. Of course not. But others — Leon Trotsky, for example — have explained it, in rational historical and sociological terms; and also in terms of the basic ideas of Marxism and of those Marxists — the Bolsheviks — who proclaimed, even when leading the Russian workers to the taking of state power in 1917, that Russia was not ripe for socialism. Where did Stalinism come from? Stalinism was a counter-revolution (on the basis of maintaining the state-owned property forms established by the revolution, developed and extended) by a distinct social formation which emerged in the '20s — a bureaucracy rooted initially in the state created for self-defence in the civil war and the wars against the 14 capitalist states which intervened in Russia. In the course of the struggle for survival in the three years after the revolution, the working class itself was dispersed and partly destroyed as a social formation, so great was the disruption caused by counterrevolutionary violence and invasion.

More: Russia in 1917 was too backward for socialism. The Russian labour movement expected that the workers of Germany and France would soon follow where they had led, and that a European socialist federation would emerge, at the heart of which would be the advanced countries whose material development and culture were on a level sufficiently high to make an advanced post-capitalist socialist society possible. But instead of joining the Russian working class in a push for socialism, the main leaders of the labour movement sustained capitalism. In Germany they did not scruple to shoot down the revolutionary workers to make Germany safe for capitalism (no more than government minister Michael Foot scrupled to use the armed power of the British state to keep Des Warren in jail for three of the last Labour government's five years in office).

Stalinist totalitarianism, with its terror and unrestrained violence, its lies and its wiping out of many of the fruits of the entire epoch of capitalist civilisation, was the system that emerged when the bureaucracy that clustered around the state in backward, isolated and ruined Russia threw off the constraints which survived from the revolutionary period and made itself master of society. The totalitarian system is the system of their unbridled rule over society and over the working class. It used the most terrible and savage violence to destroy the power of the workers and to wipe out the Russian labour movement — and the revolutionaries too. It used the power thus established and consolidated to exercise an immense totalitarian dominance in society.

The facts about that bloody Stalinist counter-revolution, which included the public trial in person or in absentia (Trotsky) of nearly all the leaders of the revolution, are very well known by now. The river of blood that marks off Stalinism from Bolshevism is by now so well charted that even Foot's beloved *Tribune*, which fellow-travelled with the Stalinists until as late as 1939, long ago became aware of it.

What sense therefore can there be in pretending that murderer and victim, Cain and Abel, Bolshevik workers' revolution and Stalinist bureaucratic counter-revolution are identical? In terms of historical fact, what sense is there in pretending that the workers' revolution of 1917, one of the great liberating events in history, directly freeing the workers, peasants and oppressed nationalities of the vast Tsarist empire, is the selfsame thing as the vile counter-revolutionary system that was erected on the political grave of that revolution, and on the graves of countless Russian workers and peasants?

There is no sense to it, nor logic, nor rational evaluation of the facts of the anti-working class counter-revolution by way of which, and out of which, the Stalinist system emerged and displaced the workers' democracy of 1917. Foot's notion that the violence of the workers' militia in 1917 is the root of the Stalinist totalitarian system is at root a religious notion (appropriate accompaniment to his fetishism of the existing form of parliamentary democracy in Britain!).

The taboo is violated and everything thereafter is contaminated, cursed, doomed. The Russian workers — not to speak of the Poles and others — today are still paying for the sins of their revolutionary mothers and fathers and grandparents 65 years ago! And Foot says he is an atheist, believe it or not!

Even if it could plausibly be argued that certain institutions set up by the Bolsheviks in the terrible struggle for survival in civil war and the war against the 14 intervening states contributed to the degeneration of the revolution and the emergence of Stalinism, it would only follow from this that certain mistakes were made, not that the revolution was itself a mistake. It would not follow that democratic mass working class action to take power and disarm the ruling class necessarily leads to totalitarianism.

The truth is the very opposite. If the Russian workers had an armed militia system now, totalitarianism would not survive a week in the USSR. If the Polish strike pickets who guarded the gates in Gdansk during the great strike of August 1980, carrying pick-axe handles, had gone on to organise an armed workers' militia then Jaruzelski's martial law in December 1981 would have been impossible. If the British trade union movement had an armed militia now, then Britain would be a much safer place for democracy than in fact it is.

Or would armed resistance by the Polish or USSR workers, even against Stalinism, also be a breach of the taboos of Foot's pacifist god? The conclusion from Stalinism, says Foot, is "the necessity of establishing some truly independent parliamentary institutions". This, he says, is the course Solidarnosc would have wished to follow in Poland. Yes! In August 1980, the most democratic parliament ever to meet in Poland lived and functioned for a month in Gdansk.

It was not a parliament like the one bound by the five year rule which sustains Mrs Thatcher. It was a workers' council, a sort of "soviet", composed of factory delegates from the entire region, who reported back to their electors and could easily be replaced. It was counterposed to the bureaucratic state apparatus, and incompatible with it and with the bureaucrats served by it. Such a system of intense democratic self-rule is always and everywhere incompatible with the rule of a stable bureaucratic state machine behind the scenes. That is why, though it was a parliament, it belonged to the type of the 1917 workers' councils, and not to the type of Michael Foot's revered institution.

Just as he invokes the dead, safe, radical causes of the past, and falsely appropriates them for use against those who stand in their living continuity, Foot misuses the Polish experience. For that tremendously democratic "parliament" in Gdansk could only have been developed and consolidated as a revolutionary movement. It could live only if it could find the force to disarm the Polish state and successfully raise the cry of national revolt against Russian overlordship in Poland (and the rest of Eastern Europe: only a movement spreading across Eastern Europe could hope to defy and defeat the Russian state).

Instead, the workers' movement, the unchallengeable power in Poland in August 1980, decided to bow to the fact of Russia's overlordship of Poland, and the consequent rule of the Polish Stalinist bureaucracy. It transformed itself into a "trade union" — though in fact Solidarnosc was always much more. And the forces of Stalinist reaction gathered strength for the blow they struck last December, when martial law was declared. What would Foot have advocated in Poland? Reliance on the Sejm (the official parliament — which showed some life, in fact)? A long, moderately conducted war of attrition — perhaps for decades — to make the Sejm "a real parliament"? There is more than one way to "sacrifice generations", Michael Foot! I repeat: the only guarantee against counter-revolution in Poland would have been an armed working class which overthrew the bureaucracy and secured Polish independence. The road to democracy in Eastern Europe and the USSR — surely even Michael Foot will have to agree — is the road of armed revolt.

The only sure guarantee against capitalist or Stalinist counter-revolution is active, self-controlling mass democracy in real control — without a reserve military force which is the iron hand in the parliamentary glove, and which the ruling class (or ruling bureaucracy) can use to strike down the masses and their democracy.

Chapter 4: Superstition or the class struggle?

The search for the original sin of Bolshevism has exercised tired and demoralised socialists for at least 50 years. Like characters in an ancient Greek drama, they seek the explanation for the Stalinist plague in some violated taboo. Was not the sin in the way the Bolshevik Party organised itself? That has always been a popular explanation, and shows signs of life now among some tired ex-radicals in the Labour Party and on its fringes. For Foot, the great sin was revolutionary violence. The diagnosis of what exactly was Bolshevism's original sin may vary, but the very notion that there was an original sin, a single flaw which contaminated everything else, has led most of its devotees away from rational socialist politics and effectively to the conclusion that the great sin of the Russian workers was to dare to take power at all. The great sin of the revolution was... the revolution.

This is Foot's conclusion, as it must be the conclusion of anyone who accepts bourgeois democracy as the culmination of historical progress. In fact, of course, Foot's method of argument is incompatible with serious historical analysis; reducing the question to one of broken taboos, it leads straight to a superstitious approach to politics, and away from a rational account of what went wrong — and what must now be done to put it right.

Inevitably, it leads to irrationality in current politics too. Foot's compulsion now to submit to Thatcher in the name of high democratic principle is as irrational as anything you will find on the hysteria-prone "revolutionary" left! For if you think, even subconsciously, in terms of broken taboos and look for some original sin committed by the revolutionary working class to explain Stalinist totalitarianism, then you must tread carefully! You don't know where the hidden taboos, curses and voodoos may be lying in wait for you!

"Democracy" is seen outside of history and imagined to be miraculously raised above the struggle of classes in history. (So too for Michael Foot is totalitarianism, as we will see.) For the future there is a terror of blundering into worse than we have now. For the present, the existing, hollowed-out British bourgeois democracy is fetishised into a decadent set of constitutional rules, forms and regulations which must be treated with reverent superstition. Socialism as a distinct system to replace capitalism is, according to this view, an "apocalyptic" dream: and you will probably end up in the nightmare of the Stalinist gulag if you dare to strike out from the rules and constraints of the existing British parliamentary system.

Even when that system allows the sustained and savage tyranny against millions of people which the Thatcher government is legally inflicting, the working class must still submit, lest worse things follow from a resistance that overflows the hallowed constitutional channels of the sacred system. For no earthly power has the right to suborn an anointed British prime minister until her full five years are up!

In Britain now, the conclusion from the idea that the working class cannot take state power, and should not try, has to be this: the last class with the historic right to fight for power and to take power was the bourgeoisie — back in the 17th century. Why the curse against perpetrators of revolutionary violence has not jinxed the British system this last 300 years, Foot forgets to explain to us. He will not be able to explain it to himself either: one does not reason with one's fetish! You chant the mantra and contemplate the holy relics, touch wood, be glad it still works, and move on, spitting contemptuous curses at the unbelievers and threats at the heretics.

In the 1930s the effete bourgeois liberals and their radical understudies repelled the rebel youth who were being ground down by the capitalist crisis. Some went over to fascism. Those who thought they were choosing communism found Stalinist totalitarianism acceptable in part because of revulsion against Foot-style worship of passivity cloaked in commitment to formal democracy. The disintegration of society seemed to show the impotence and irrelevance of democracy. Democracy had either to be renewed and continued as a weapon of socialists fighting to re-make society or sink into discredit along with capitalism.

There is a fine scene in one of Luis Bunuel's films. A woman sits in a chair, and a man, a fetishist, crouches in front of her, fondling her leg, putting it against his face, kissing it. His sexuality is expressed in this way because in his subconscious the fetish has taken on all the meaning that other people find in a partner's body. The man is experiencing his ecstasy, locked into a private world — and the woman finds it impossible to suppress a big bored yawn. The symbolic links in the man's subconscious, rooted in childhood memories and associations (and childish misapprehensions) mean that her leg has the power to trigger his emotions. But they can't mean anything to her. They exist only in his private world.

That is how the legalistic concerns of Michael Foot's political ancestors appeared to the radical youth in the '30s. And today the Parliamentary

Labour Party are not active, creative, improvising fighters of a living democracy but tired worshippers of an ancient fetish to which they will willingly sacrifice the living stream of youth — because they have forgotten what the struggle for democracy was all about in the first place! They do not notice how badly their beloved parliament has fallen into disrepair, how deficient it all now is as a living democracy. They are unable even to face up to the questions about British democracy posed to honest democrats by what the minority-based Thatcher government is now using parliament to legally do to this "generation".

They are obsessed with their own symbols and reminiscences of the infancy of parliamentary democracy. The labour movement has its own concerns. In the here and now, the PLP fails to speak to more and more workers about the things that concern them. That is why the Labour Party is in crisis. In the present condition of Britain, either democracy will be linked with an effective programme of socialist transformation, or democracy will be radically undermined and discredited.

Foot's view of Stalinism is all of a piece with his views and perspectives for Britain, and his self-avowed Fabian politics. Foot — in 1982! — does not understand that Stalinist totalitarianism is the rule of a distinct social formation. Neither does he understand that the British parliamentary system is a shield and an instrument for the rule of a distinct social class. There is no more blatant example of Foot's class blindness for British politics than his inability to understand who rules in the USSR — the fact that totalitarianism arises because a minority rules over the vast oppressed majority (and therefore, Comrade Foot, it follows that totalitarianism is simply inconceivable as the instrument of a self-ruling working class majority).

The truth is, Foot himself has an elitist conception of "socialism" — a civilised Fabian elitism which he contrasts with Stalinism, and Thatcherism, but elitism, nonetheless. Condemning Stalinism's sacrifice of generations, he insists on the need "to let them establish for themselves what may be the nature and scale of the sacrifice". But this shows he has missed the point. In a socialist democracy no elite would "let" the people decide matters: no-one else but the people could decide.

And when Foot contrasts his view of socialism to trade union direct action, the elitism is again clear: "Increasingly as the years passed, he [Aneurin Bevan] placed his confidence in collectivist, social power, to be wielded by the central state, acting through parliament, with all the devices, chances and protections of open debate which he knew so well how to exploit on behalf of... his people and his party."

But overwhelming social power always remains directly in the hands of the bourgeoisie who own factories, banks, newspapers and TV stations. The social power wielded by the central state is now in the hands of Thatcher — who got a minority of the votes cast in 1979 — and who is using that power, Jacobin fashion, to strike terrible blows at the working class and at the organised labour movement. Backed by the social power of the bourgeoisie, Thatcher is using the central state power to conduct naked, open, vindictive class warfare.

And Foot is using these arguments now to dissuade the labour movement from taking direct action to defend itself. Only the elite and the elite institutions — crowned by parliament — have the right of initiative. The working class does not have even the right of resistance to tyranny. When Foot accuses us of being anti-democratic, he takes his own elitist and bureaucratic — and parliamentarian — concept of socialism and accuses the Marxists of wanting to realise it too rapidly, too brutally and too completely.

When the Fabian looks at Stalinism, he is looking at himself in a distorting mirror — or rather in a different historical dimension. The Fabians recognise in Stalinism a development in a barren climate of their own "socialism". Most now recoil in horror, though others, like the Webbs in the 1930s, embraced Stalinism for its family likeness to themselves. The statist "socialisms" of Fabians and Stalinists are cousins if not twins. Both rest on the rule of an elite over the masses (in Britain, with a five-year release mechanism).

The Marxist programme — of Marx, Engels, Lenin and Trotsky — has always, from the 1880s at least, stood in sharp contrast to the state socialism to which both the Fabians and their monstrous cousin, Stalinism, belong on the level of ideas. Marxism proposes socialisation of the means of production to be achieved by the working class and to be administered by and for that class. As a precondition for the healthy development of the socialist society, there is to be no state in the old sense.

The workers' state is not Stalinist collectivism, a tyrannical all-controlling state which is the instrument of the bureaucracy against the people and especially against the working class. Nor is it any version of the existing state collectivism of the Fabians, writ large or modified. Socialist transformation by the working class will only be possible if it is linked to an expansion of liberty: "every cook shall govern", as Lenin put it. When the supposedly anti-democratic Marxists advocate something other than parliamentary democracy, this expansion of liberty is what they advocate.

The present type of parliamentary democracy is organically tied to the old historical form of state power — rule of society by minorities, typically through bureaucracies. Socialism needs the destruction of that form of state power. If the bureaucratic form of state power were fused with control of the wealth-producing activities of society, then it could, even in a relatively rich society like Britain, lead to corruption, inefficiency, and abuse of power, perhaps even to a bureaucratic dictatorship. So Foot, Kinnock, etc. are right to beware of themselves and their socialism! But they should not attribute it to us.

In the view of Marxists, such a qualitative expansion of democracy in the running of society lies at the other side of a socialist revolution which overthrows capitalism (and, in the Stalinist states, the bureaucracy). But that revolution is in turn inconceivable except as the culmination of a great explosion of working class democracy and of struggles to defend, expand and deepen democracy.

Workers' socialist revolution would undoubtedly present itself to the ruling class and its hangers-on as highly authoritarian, but to the mass of the people as a great expansion of democratic self-rule. This paradox merely expresses the fact that our society is divided into two antagonistic classes, one of which must go down so that the other can rise.

In sum, then, Foot's difference with unfalsified Marxism over democracy is that he is himself a mere bourgeois democrat and an elitist, who counterposes the limited accomplishments of bourgeois democracy to the necessary future development of democracy which the working class must achieve if it is itself ever to rule directly in society. More: he has abandoned the notion of developing and deepening democracy, and maybe never understood the revolutionary Marxist goal of developing democracy beyond the present system into social and economic self-rule and self-administration.

There are two distinct but interwoven strands in the attitudes the labour movement has taken to parliamentary democracy. The first was and is ardent championing of parliamentary democracy and democratic liberties. In varying alliances with sections of the middle class, early labour movements fought to extend the suffrage and enlarge the power of parliament — often by revolutionary means.

The first mass political labour movement, Chartism, took shape around demands for the reshaping of the existing parliamentary system so as to admit the working class to the suffrage and make it possible for workers to be MPs. In Britain, as late as 1917, the Workers' Socialist Federation, led by Sylvia Pankhurst (emerging out of the Workers' Suffrage Federation, which in turn came out of the left wing of the suffragette movement in the East End) based themselves on an extremely radical programme of democratic reform, attempting to graft on to the British parliament features of the workers' council system that had just emerged in Russia.

In 1934 Trotsky suggested a united front with reformist workers in France for a similar programme.

"As long as the majority of the working class continues on the basis of bourgeois democracy, we are ready to defend it with all our forces against violent attacks from the Bonapartist and fascist bourgeoisie.

However, we demand from our class brothers who adhere to 'democratic' socialism that they be faithful to their ideas, that they draw inspiration from the ideas and methods not of the Third Republic but of the Convention of 1793. Down with the Senate, which is elected by limited suffrage, and which renders the power of universal suffrage a mere illusion! Down with the presidency of the republic, which serves as a hidden point of concentration for the forces of militarism and reaction!

A single assembly must combine the legislative and executive powers. Members would be elected for two years, by universal suffrage at eighteen years of age, with no discrimination of sex or nationality. Deputies would be elected on the basis of local assemblies, constantly revocable by their constituents, and would receive the salary of a skilled worker. This is the only measure that would lead the masses forward instead of pushing them backward. A more generous democracy would facilitate the struggle for workers' power.

We want to attain our objective not by armed conflicts between the various groups of toilers, but by real workers' democracy, by propaganda and loyal criticism, by the voluntary regrouping of the great majority of the proletariat under the flag of true communism. Workers adhering to democratic socialism must further understand that it is not enough to defend democracy; democracy must be regained.

The moving of the political centre of gravity from parliament towards the cabinet, from the cabinet towards the oligarchy of finance capital, generals, police, is an accomplished fact. Neither the present parliament nor the new elections can change this.

We can defend the whole sorry remains of democracy, and especially we can enlarge the democratic arena for the activity of the masses, only by annihilating the armed fascist forces that, on 6 February 1934, started moving the axis of the state and are still doing so. "

The second strand has consisted of a drive to create new, different, specifically working class organs of democracy — either by converting old forms to the purpose, or by establishing completely new ones. The Paris Commune in 1871 was an example of the taking over of old forms — the Paris City council! The creation of new forms began in St Petersburg, Russia, in 1905, when striking workers who did not have political rights elected their own local parliament or council of workers' deputies — the "soviet".

After the overthrow of Tsarism in February 1917, a vast network of such soviets developed, pyramids of city, district, and all-Russian gatherings. In their own way, from the ground up, the soviets realised such old working class demands as direct control of the legislature — delegates could be recalled and replaced, easily and repeatedly. The soviet network showed itself to be a uniquely flexible and responsive system of democratic self-organisation and, increasingly, of self-rule by the Russian masses. Whereas even the most democratic parliamentary system was tied to the bourgeois military/bureaucratic structure, the soviets were radically counterposed to the surviving Tsarist military/bureaucratic state.

In 1917 the Congress of Soviets (with the Bolshevik Party as its driving force) seized state power. Thereafter the drive to reform and develop the existing parliaments gave place, for millions of revolutionary workers throughout the world, to a commitment to soviets as the highest form of democracy. Everywhere on earth, revolutionary-minded people recognised the soviet as the working class form of democracy.

Commitment to soviets became a central part of the programme of revolutionary socialism.

"Soviet" meant, then, workers' councils within which there would be a plurality of "soviet" parties. Nobody in the communist movement advocated the idea that soviets would be ruling organs of state in a one-party system. Through most of the civil war in Russia and the wars of intervention, non-Bolshevik parties loyal to the workers' state — J. Martov's Menshevik Internationalists, for example — were legally active in the soviets. When, in March 1921, at the end of the civil war, the Bolsheviks banned all other Soviet parties, it was a temporary measure, not the norm of working class rule. Not long after the Stalinists seized control: one party rule became the norm. Inevitably this Russian reality confused many communists as to exactly what soviet rule would be.

The result was to banish concern with democracy and to falsify the very language and concepts in which both the old pre-world war socialist movement, and the early communist movement, had understood democracy. In consequence, "communism" had, partly through confusion and incoherence, arising out of anti-social-democratic polemic, an anti-democratic bias, even before full-blown Stalinism.

After the full-scale Stalinist counter-revolution in the late '20s, the one-party system was proclaimed as the true working class democracy, universally applicable. The basic programmatic norms of revolutionary socialism were being pulped and destroyed. Democratic ideals and goals that had been central to radical thought since the French Revolution or even since the English revolutions of the 17th century, were replaced — though the old democratic labels were still used — by realities which concentrated in themselves the statism and authoritarianism which different embodiments of the left had been fighting for hundreds of years! Mystification and confusion inevitably followed.

Meanwhile, in the hands of the right wing of the international labour movement, the commitment to perfecting the democratic institutions of capitalist society became a commitment to the bourgeoisie against the revolutionary workers and their soviets. In German the 1918 revolution created a bourgeois democratic regime, realising most of the "democratic" demands of the old workers' movement, but as part of a landlord-bourgeois counter-revolution against the workers, the right wing socialists allied with the Junkers against the revolutionary workers!

This prostitution by the right wing socialists of the old socialist ideals of enlarging democracy convinced revolutionary workers that only soviet democracy could serve socialist ends. It also softened them up to receive the Stalinist revelations that all the old talk of democracy meant nothing but bourgeois lies. It helped ease them into acceptance of the one-party Stalinist totalitarian state as the true proletarian democracy.

In the mid-'30s the Stalinists dropped soviets from their programme and, pursuing alliances with the right of the labour movements and with liberals to serve Russian foreign policy interests, became hypocritical worshippers of the existing parliaments. At the same time they pushed the debilitating lie that Stalinist totalitarianism was a form of "workers" democracy. This senseless assertion became an article of faith for two generations of revolutionary workers. The basic idea that socialists must continue to struggle for human liberty and freedom was expunged from the programme of "communism". "Democracy" — like "socialism" —

became a cynical catch-cry, shot through with double-think about the "democracy" of the society where the Stalinist bureaucrats ruled.

Trotsky noted the corrupting effect of this on the labour movement itself when he commented on the Norwegian Labour Party: "I soon had occasion to become convinced, by experience, that the old bourgeois functionaries sometimes have a broader viewpoint and a more profound sense of dignity than Messrs 'Socialist' Ministers... "

In the class struggle, however, despite both reformists and Stalinists, embattled workers throw up soviet-type structures. Since 1917, soviets — workers' councils elected from factories and districts — have been thrown up in a large number of countries in conditions of large-scale working class struggle. From Austria, Germany and Hungary in 1918, and Hungary again in 1956, through to Gdansk in 1980, soviets have emerged as flexible forms of working class democratic self-organisation — factory committees generalised to the whole of society. The historical experience of soviets as a form of social rule is, of course, limited. Even in the most advanced case, that of Russia, where soviets became the cellular structure of the new workers' state, the soviets had little time to evolve or develop and articulate institutions for the detailed running of society.

The bourgeoisie in countries like Britain has had centuries to evolve their parliaments and law courts and divisions of power. We had a single year! And the civil war and invading armies stifled the soviets. Stalin buried them. As early as the end of 1918 the soviets in the USSR were being undermined as freely functioning democratic organs by the exigencies of civil war. They were shortly to be gutted of all real life. This process culminated in the ban on every party but the Bolsheviks in March 1921. Intended as a temporary civil war measure, it became fixed, as we have seen, as the norm of the Stalinist political counter-revolution.

Nevertheless it is clear:

• That these soviets, which have emerged in vastly different conditions and countries, are not accidental forms. At the very least they are valuable organs of working class self-organisation in struggle.

• In Russia before they were blasted by civil war, they were a form of democracy more flexible, adjustable and responsive than any other "parliamentary" system. And, for the sake of clarifying things in the British labour movement, it is important to be clear that soviets are a "parliamentary" system only with a more direct democracy, the right of recall, etc.

• Being independent of the existing bureaucratic/military system to which capitalist rule is tied, they are — to go by experience so far — the best form of organisation for a workers' movement that is seriously setting about transforming society against the will of the ruling class.

• That they are more appropriate than any other known form of democracy for the socialist rule of the working class, in so far as it involves a qualitative expansion of the direct exercise of democracy.

• That they can and will re-emerge at intensive levels of mass working class action, when the struggle overflows the channels of the existing system. We may have come close to it in Britain in 1972.

This is why workers' councils are a central part of the programme of revolutionary Marxism. The word "soviet" has been utterly debased by association with the totalitarian bureaucracy of the USSR — which, as the sour old joke has it, contains four lies in its name: it is not a union, there are no soviets, it is not socialist, and it is not a republic. But Marxists remain committed to soviet democracy. We continue the old socialist commitment to expanding democracy in a qualitative way. We explain the limits of existing democracy and the possibilities of a different democracy.

Is this Marxist commitment counterposed to the basic labour movement commitment to parliamentary democracy? Not at all. Socialism is not possible until the mass of workers want it and are prepared to realise it — neither is an extension of democracy beyond the level already attained. It is in the direct interests of the working class to defend the existing system against anti-democratic attacks. It is in our interest to extend it and better it (for example by making the next Labour prime minister subject to election by the labour movement, outside of parliament; by freeing the existing system from the dead grip of the parliamentary oligarchy of the PLP; and by ensuring that there is some relationship between what aspirant MPs and aspirant majority parties say they will do, and what they actually do). All this is the difference between good and bad circulation in the existing body politic.

Thus Marxists have much in common with people in the labour movement whose best notion of democracy is parliamentary democracy. We can agree to fight to rejuvenate the existing system; we could agree to defend it with guns against, for example, a military coup. Marxists can and do form such alliances with honest "non-soviet" democrats. The reason why we cannot and do not form such relations with the right wing and the soft left is not because we are not democrats, but because they are very bad democrats. They worship the miserably inadequate system that exists.

They have done more than any Marxist to educate sections of the labour movement about the limits of parliamentary democracy: they have even exaggerated those limits and made them far more narrow than they would be for a fighting labour movement intent on defending the working class interest. They have, in successive Labour governments, and especially since 1964, done more than anyone else to discredit parliamentary democracy and render cynical large sections of the labour movement. This cynicism has corroded not only democracy but the political consciousness of the labour movement. Marxists, while we tell the workers who listen to us that they should rely only on their own strength, see no advantage or gain for our politics in cynicism about politics, or even about the existing parliament.

While small groups can advance to a higher understanding by way of such disillusionment, the great mass of the labour movement is thrown back by it. The mass of the labour movement will advance to a better understanding of the limits of parliamentary democracy, not by pure disgust with the Labour right — that is a passive, politically limited response — but most likely by class struggle which includes attempts to use to the very maximum the existing institutions of the labour movement and of British bourgeois democracy.

How might soviets emerge in Britain? When you look concretely at how the existing British parliamentary system might be displaced by workers' councils, the difference between Marxist democrats and the burnt-out parliamentarians becomes clear. The difference between what we really stand for and the lies they tell about us become clear.

Propaganda by Marxists will not by itself win enough workers to support for workers' councils ("soviets") to threaten the parliamentary system. The relevant historical experience on which the proposal is based is too remote. Propaganda alone could not win the mass of workers away from commitment to the existing parliamentary system.

Even if it is partly eroded, belief in the parliamentary system is still very deep and powerful in the British people and the labour movement. And the system still has a lot of flexibility. Soviets have most often emerged in conditions where parliamentary democracy did not exist, or was severely limited. The precondition for soviets in Britain to move from the realm of propaganda and accounts of history to the realm of practical working class politics would be — obviously — mass struggle, but also and centrally a major erosion of belief that parliament is an accessible democratic institution.

Councils of Action having many points in common with soviets came into existence in Britain in 1920. Something like an incipient soviet emerged in Durham during the 1926 General Strike. But even if a vast network of Councils of Action were now to emerge in a general strike, it is unlikely that they would starkly counterpose themselves to the existing system, as an alternative system of democratic rule — unless there were a serious erosion of belief in parliament as the democratic system. The use of parliamentary elections would be a major weapon of the ruling class and of the right with which to derail and demobilise any general strike movement. That is what they did in France in 1968.

How will such an erosion of belief in Westminster occur? Even if a large revolutionary Marxist party existed, it could not occur, I repeat, as a result of propaganda alone. It will only occur when the ruling class — in response to the exigencies of the struggle against the working class to keep or exert control — is forced to begin to abrogate its own system, to downgrade it, thereby, over time, robbing its processes of credibility. Thus the existing system would have to be undermined from two sides — by growing self-confidence, self-organisation, and disillusionment with parliament among the working class, and by growing impatience or desperation among the ruling class.

This is what Marxists such as Trotsky teach us on this question. I have already quoted Trotsky's call to the social reformist workers of France to defend parliamentary democracy (1934). In the same vein he warned Marxists not to make a religion of soviets. This advice has one hundred times greater force today, when the experience of the initial liberating Russian soviets is so far back in history. "Soviets" now are, and can only be, a matter of propaganda: and the socialist who would counterpose such propaganda to the necessary working class struggle, which must include struggles around the existing parliamentary system, is a sectarian fool, incapable of learning either from life or from Trotsky's approach in France.

Now, if the Marxist expectation that the ruling class will not be bound by its own parliamentary rules is wrong, then very probably "soviets" will remain a matter of propaganda by Marxists who favour soviets as a different, better system of democracy. In that case, the right and the soft left, who now witch-hunt those who advocate a different form of democracy as enemies of democracy, have little to worry about.

They worry, in fact, because they are not quite naive liberals. Foot, in his *Observer* articles, talked of the danger of the "storm-troopers". He says that the left gains from the parliamentary niceties because the right has a tradition of fighting and the left does not. He knows the political facts of life, but he lacks the socialist seriousness to try to call new facts into being — like the fact of a working class militia, for example.

What do we do when the bourgeoisie does begin to disrupt democracy and attack it? The labour movement will fight back. We will not abandon bourgeois democracy or democratic rights. Soviets may well arise in defence of parliamentary democracy — as the only way to continue what was valuable in bourgeois democracy, when it is abandoned by the bourgeoisie as the class struggle escalates.

We will defend democratic rights tooth and nail, and with guns. Most of the right wing "professional democrats" won't. The German Social Democrats helped the Junker army to massacre revolutionary workers in 1919 under the banner of preserving parliamentary democracy: they meekly surrendered it to Hitler in 1933. The Party leader in the Reichstag, Otto Wels, meekly offered his and his party's collaboration to Hitler, who didn't need it then.

So it is not our propaganda for a different sort of democracy, soviets, that worries the right, nor is it only that we lack respect for "Parliament". It is not even entirely a matter of grabbing a convenient demarcation line to serve an organisational purpose now. What is it then that worries them? What is the dividing line between them and us? The dividing line is extraparliamentary struggle now. Their main target is not Trotskyists making propaganda for soviets, it is the serious reformist left. They are using the witch-hunt against the allegedly anti-democratic Trotskyists as a means of frightening the less determined section of the left out of any will that Labour and the unions should fight the Tories now, using extraparliamentary action where appropriate.

The print union SOGAT is now proposing strike action in open, proud defiance of the Tory anti-union laws. Are the leaders of the Labour Party seriously proposing to rule out such action? Are they seriously proposing that the labour movement should allow itself to be crippled? Yes, they are! Their fire is directed now at those who want to fight back. They prefer to counterpose the existing parliamentary system to the needs of the living labour movement. They stand for an exaggeratedly slavish legalism — and against resistance to a government that is an outrage against the spirit of even bourgeois democracy.

Their rallying cry, "democracy", is a double lie because they will not fight back against Thatcher even to defend the democracy they now hide behind against the criticism of the Marxists. It is the "anti-democratic" Marxists who want to defend trade union rights and democracy against Thatcher, not the professional democrats!

We have heard Foot's canting, his denunciation of what he thinks is a certain form of socialism — though in fact he is dealing with Stalinism, the rule of a distinct social bureaucracy, and not with any form of socialism — in the now fashionable bourgeois-liberal formula which faults Stalinism for "sacrificing generations". But in Britain now, it is the socialists who reject Michael Foot's fetish of the existing forms of parliamentary democracy, or at least reject the rules that would sanctify Thatcher's work as the distillate of pure parliamentary democracy, who oppose the "sacrifice of generations".

It is Foot and his friends who are willing to sacrifice this generation of British young people! Unlike Foot, we can conceive of a different and better society, and we think the labour movement should fight for it. Politically prostrate, Foot can only hope for a new, tepid Labour government, to do things more humanely than Thatcher.

Foot is no longer even notionally a socialist: his programme now is not that of a socialist, but that of a liberal humanitarian administration of capitalism. He wants to soften the blows of British capitalism's decline, but no doubt will be willing again to obey the dictats of the IMF, and to make secret deals to sustain the state apparatus of potential violence against the working class. That is the grand conclusion from his great historical excursion into Stalinism — don't go for "remote ends" or a different system, go for a new middle-of-the-road or right wing Labour administration.

He is willing to bowdlerise the living historical process by abstracting from it the struggles of socialists for a socialist solution to the present convulsions of British capitalism. He talks of the "treason" of those on the left whom he says are now reconciled to defeat in the next election. But it is the witch-hunters who are willing to gut the party to make it safe for themselves to commit this treason. The left is not reconciled to electoral defeat.

There is another, and more deadly, sort of defeat, though — inner political defeatism such as Foot's which abandons the very goal of socialism and disguises this with a great show of commitment to electoral victory.

Foot's reasoning, and its conclusion of hopelessness, passivity, fetish worship and superstitious dread of action, offers nothing to the working class movement now, or to socialism, or to "democracy". Our great tragedy is that Foot and his friends are the incumbent leaders of the labour movement. Their passivity threatens us with disaster. It is a major factor now on Thatcher's side in the class struggle.

The Italian Marxist Antonio Gramsci, who was destroyed in a Mussolini jail, put it all very clearly long ago: "Reality is the result of the application of wills to the society of things... to put aside every voluntary effort and calculate only the intervention of other wills as an objective element in the general game is to mutilate reality itself. Only those who strongly want to do it identify the necessary element for the realisation of their will." (*The Modern Prince*, my emphasis). By their self-effacing passivity, their refusal to lead the labour movement in a fightback now, Foot and his friends mutilate reality. They help Thatcher and encourage her.

What do we need to do instead? Thatcher's drastic action for the ruling class needs to be met with drastic working class action in self-defence and in pursuit of our own interests. The labour movement needs to rouse itself into a campaign to bring down this undemocratic and anti-working class government!

The labour movement desperately needs a perspective of hope and a belief in the possibility of an alternative system. The labour movement needs to have its vague commitment to socialism honed sharp and clear; it needs to rededicate itself to the fight for a more representative, more flexible and more real democracy than this one.

Only the struggle for a workers' government which will base itself on the roused and active masses of the working class — that is, on mass workers' democracy — offers a road out of Britain's impasse. Only a labour movement which is willing and eager to use its strength in industry and on the streets to challenge the government, and to deny its claims to democratic validity, will be able to rally the forces to carve out that road.

The Conway Hall debate (1994)
Democracy and direct action

Do official Labour politics offer any real hope today? Or must serious socialists, and even serious democrats, look instead to the revolutionary left? Such was the question in debate before a packed audience at London's Conway Hall on Wednesday 9 March 1994, when Sean Matgamna, editor of *Socialist Organiser*, a paper banned by the Labour Party leaders in 1990 for our Trotskyist politics, confronted Michael Foot, leader of the Labour Party from 1980 to 1983.

Sean Matgamna accused the Labour Party leadership of paving the way for Thatcherism and then succumbing to it.

In 1974 a wave of industrial action brought down the Tory Government, and we got a Labour government. "That Labour government did not act even as a serious reformist government. It carried through some superficial reforms, but fundamentally it prepared the way for Thatcherism by demobilising the working class and beginning the process of cuts.

"But even in 1979-81 our movement was still very strong. We could have driven Thatcher from office as we drove Heath from office.

"Why didn't we? There was a tiredness in the movement, after what the Labour government had done, at the same time as a terrible slump and mass unemployment. But crucially the leaders of the labour movement surrendered. They surrendered in the most shameful way.

"The Labour and trade-union leaders accepted that the Tories had to rule, that we could not resist Parliament. They allowed the Tories to ride roughshod over our class".

Sean Matgamna quoted the anarchist Errico Malatesta, warning of what would happen in Italy after 1919-20, when workers occupied the factories and the bosses held on to power only "by the skin of their teeth". "If we let this auspicious moment escape us, we shall have to pay one day in tears of blood for the fear which we now inspire in the middle class".

The British working class, said Matgamna, has been "paying for the last 15 years for the fear which we inspired in the ruling class in the 1970s, because the Labour and trade union leaders have failed to fight — again and again.

"They did not defend even their own welfare state. They were driven down a whole decade running before the Tories, until today the Labour leaders are not at all easy to distinguish from the Tories.

"They accept much of what the Tories have done to the National Health Service. Over the last 15 years the Tories have passed anti-union laws which have left Britain with the least free trade-union movement in Europe. Have the Labour leaders said they will reverse those laws, and restore freedom of action to the working class? No, they have not. They have said that they will leave on the statute book substantial parts of what the Tories have done.

"I never felt for the old right-wing Labour leaders like Hugh Gaitskell, such hatred and contempt as I feel for the Labour leaders now. They are not honest reformists. They are people who kow-tow to the Tories, gutless and shameless. They have forgotten everything except power — no, not power, office!"

In the early 1980s, Matgamna recalled, *Socialist Organiser* had argued for the labour movement to mobilise direct action to stop the Tories, right across the country, in every area possible. People like Michael Foot argued that such action was "not democratic".

"Their conception of democracy", argued Matgamna, "is far too limited. Even the bourgeois-democratic revolutions in America and France proclaimed the right of revolt against tyrannical governments. And the Thatcher government was a tyrannical government, despite its majority in Parliament.

"Democracy is real self-rule. In Britain we do not have real self rule. One of the great achievements of the bourgeoisie over the last 150 years has been to take the idea of democracy, which people had understood to mean not just political democracy but also social democracy, and empty it out.

"Democracy today is accepted to be merely shallow political democracy. At work, decisions that affect our lives radically and fundamentally are made not democratically but by the capitalists.

"We need a struggle to extend democracy. We should start now with a fight for free trade unions".

Michael Foot explained that he had accepted the invitation to debate "because of the name of Leon Trotsky — one of the great socialist figures of this century, a man of action and a writer. No other socialist of this century has combined those two things so well".

Foot "deeply regretted" that in the late 1930s, when he first worked on *Tribune*, "we did not report openly and faithfully what was happening in the Moscow Trials — which was a grave departure from the original ideals of the Russian Revolution".

To Matgamna, Foot responded by defending both the record of the 1974-9 Labour government and the politics of the present Labour Party leadership.

"The 1974-9 Labour government, even with the tiny majority we had, was a very much better government than the one we had in the previous decade. We were committed to do lots of socialist things, and many of them we did carry out.

"Some of what we did you could reckon in figures. The numbers of people in trade unions in this country in 1979, when that last Labour government left office, were higher than they had ever been before.

"Or take the numbers of people in employment. I was at the Department of Employment when the number of people unemployed in this country went up over one million. I was ashamed of the situation. We tried to reverse it.

"We used a whole series of measures to do it, some short-term and some longer-term, with at least this result, that when we left office in 1979 more people in Britain were in work than ever before. And more women were in jobs, and better jobs.

"We introduced the best new Factory Act that had ever been produced for protecting workers. We extended the field of protection to some five or six million people who had never been covered by health and safety provisions before.

"For the first time in British history, we wrote into the legislation that trade unions on the spot must have the legal right to raise health and safety issues in their workplace.

"Those gains are not safe with a Tory government, and we've got to extend them much further — but they are part of industrial democracy. Extending rights to safety at work is a central part of democracy.

"We wanted to do more, but were not able to because when we lost our majority the Liberals were not prepared to vote for measures to give workers in the workshop and workplace a greatly increased influence and say. But I trust that is one of the things a new Labour government is going to do.

"Of course it was a terrible tragedy when the Tories won in 1979 and again in 1983. Some of us were trying to say to the trade unions, and everyone else: we really must stop this Thatcher lot from ever getting in. If they do get in, they are going to destroy what we have succeeded in building over the years.

"Tragically, it has happened. That does not alter the fact that warnings were given.

"Part of what we are arguing about is the methods by which democratic movements and labour movements can achieve their objectives. I am not saying, and anyone would be a fool who said, that it is only through Parliament that it can be done. But it's equally foolish to say that you don't have to worry about what happens in Parliament.

"There would not have been a Parliament with the rights we have today if it had not been for the struggles of the labour movement. It is true that one or two of the demands of the Chartist movement [of the 1830s-50s] have not been carried out — though whether annual parliaments are a good idea I'm not sure — but the others have, and it shows what can be done by democratic action over a period.

"In the Chartist movement they had lots of arguments between people who said on the one side that they must only act under the law, and on the other side the so-called physical-force people, Julian Harney and the rest. At the end, Julian Harney said that William Lovett, who put the case on the other side, was the best of them all. Harney was not giving up his own case, but he was respecting and understanding the argument between them.

"And that was when we did not have the vote, and the case of those who argued for direct action was much stronger than now, when we do have the vote. We've got to use the vote — and use it much more skilfully and aggressively. We've got to use both weapons — industrial power and political power.

"It's not true that the Labour Party is giving up the fight to defend the National Health Service. Not at all. As soon as we get a new Labour government I have not the slightest doubt that one of the very first things it will be carrying into effect will be the fullest possible re-establishment of a proper Health Service on the same socialist principles on which it was started by the 1945 Labour government."

Despite repeated criticism from the floor, Michael Foot returned to the same assertions in his summing-up. "I'm not saying that all the last Labour government did was right. But we carried through every manifesto commitment that we could carry out.

"The Labour Party are going to restore the NHS as a major part of what they do in the next government. It may not be in exactly the same form, because after all Aneurin Bevan himself wanted to make the machinery of the Health Service much more democratically controlled. I'm sure that is included in the propositions put forward by the Labour Party".

Sean Matgamna declared flatly that he did not believe Michael Foot on

Labour and the Health Service.

"That does not affect our support for Labour in elections. The Labour Party does not belong to the scoundrels who lead it, it belongs to the trade-union and working-class movement.

"For ourselves, *Socialist Organiser* was banned in 1990, and we've had people expelled, but we haven't left the Labour Party. We organise ourselves in the Alliance for Workers' Liberty, both outside the Labour Party and inside the Labour Party.

"The general lesson of the last 15 years is that you do not get stable reforms under capitalism. You cannot win stable improvements without destroying the roots of capitalism.

"The class struggle goes on. Our side has suffered defeats. But capitalism generates class struggle. There is a tremendous build-up of explosive discontent in this country. The labour movement will revive. But we must learn the lessons of the past.

"Central to our socialism is the struggle for democracy. We do not live in anything but the travesty of a democracy. We do not have democracy which is self-rule in our own lives.

"A campaign for democracy, if taken seriously, is a campaign to revive the ideas of socialism. I do not believe we can have a peaceful transition from democracy as we have it now to socialism, but nevertheless it is true that consistent democracy, applied through the whole of society, would be socialism. The democracy we have now is a hollow democracy."

Concluding, Matgamna pointed to the central and immediate question of workers' democratic rights which, he said, Michael Foot had evaded. "We no longer have a free trade union movement. The law bans working-class solidarity. We can campaign against this, and for free trade unions, and in doing so we should revive the struggle for socialism.

"We will fight back; and then we will make the ruling class pay in tears of blood for what they have done to our class over the last 15 years".

Martin Thomas, *Socialist Organiser* 593, 17 March 1994

What revolutionary socialists advocated against Thatcher

Sean Matgamna

The class struggle left in 1980

Socialist Organiser is dedicated to the following basic propositions:
• That a socialist society, in which the economy is owned collectively by the producers who live in a self-controlling and self-administering socialist democracy, is what we want as the alternative to capitalism — which is a system of exploitation of the vast majority by a small class who own the means of production They use their ownership of the means of production to extract and store up wealth for themselves, not hesitating, for example, to put two million people on the dole if it is necessary for that purpose.
• That here and now the alternatives are either the continued deterioration of the working class itself as capitalism rots around us, or such a socialist system.
• That only the working class can create such a system, by taking control of society out of the hands of the capitalists.
• That for this to become possible, the existing labour movement — Labour Party and trade unions — must transform themselves organisationally, by a process of democratisation and by breaking the undemocratic power of cliques, bureaucrats, and uncontrollable Parliamentarian elites within the organisations of the labour movement.
• That, simultaneously, the labour movement must re-arm itself politically with the ideas and the immediate goal of a revolutionary socialist transformation of society.
• That because socialism is impossible until the working class acts to realise it, and because there is only one working class and one mass labour movement, revolutionary socialists must work and organise within the existing labour movement, built by many decades and even centuries of working class struggle, to help the movement achieve this political and organisational self-renovation,
• That if those who hold to the basic ideas of revolutionary socialism

refuse to do this, they condemn themselves to sterility, by way of impotent sideline carping at the movement as it has been shaped by history so far, and to sectarian irrelevance in the irreplaceable work of changing the movement.

• That there are in stark logic only two alternatives: either to fight to change the existing labour movement, including its organic political wing, the Labour Party. Or, to adopt the project of building one's own "pure" labour movement from the ground up, in parallel to the one the working class has so far created. And therefore that those who reject the former, and, implicitly, accept the latter, are in fact pessimistic and defeatist about the prospects facing the labour movement in the next historic period... no matter how "left" and "revolutionary" be their talk and their view of what they themselves are, and however "intransigent" and "uncompromising" their denunciations of the existing labour movement are.

For if we do not, in the relatively short period ahead, succeed in reorganising and politically transforming the existing labour movement, which is the only mass labour movement, and which holds the allegiance of millions of the most advanced workers, and if we fail to win it for revolutionary socialist politics, methods, and perspectives, then the working class will face a historic defeat. Even if we kick out the Tories — as we have the strength to do, for now — we will, as in 1974, when we kicked out Heath, have only a politically bankrupt (Foot/Healey-led) labour movement as our "alternative" to the Tories.

• That therefore there is great urgency about the work of organising a non-sectarian and anti-sectarian left wing in the labour movement, to help it make itself ready to answer the needs of the situation which the working class faces as capitalism declines and rots.

Because such a left wing must unite the revolutionary left around a perspective of winning the existing labour movement to revolutionary socialism, it must also be a left wing which fights (by reason and argument) the sectarians who counterpose political shibboleths not in consonance with the class struggle or who counterpose their own organisations to those of the mass labour movement in a way which is destructive of the work that needs to be done.

In addition, *Socialist Organiser* believes:

That this left must set itself the goal of winning the labour movement to fight immediately to drive the Tories out and install a workers' government. This will differ from the Labour governments so far in being based directly on the organisations of the labour movement, being under the labour movement's direct control (at least to a serious extent), and fighting to serve the working class interest against the bourgeoisie

That the fight to democratise the labour movement — the Labour Party, and the trade unions too — is the fight to make such a Workers' Government a possibility. If we drive through the Brighton and Blackpool decisions on reselection, if we subordinate the Parliamentary Labour Party to the labour movement, and if we get a serious proportion of the votes for electing the Labour leader (i.e., if Labour has a Parliamentary majority, the Prime Minister), and if we succeed in politically re-arming the labour movement with radical working-class socialist policies, then such a government will be attainable.

From introduction to Socialist Organiser *pamphlet,*
Why we need a workers' government

Stop the Thatcher blitz!

How can the labour movement slop the full-scale offensive launched by the Thatcher government? After six months of Tory rule, sections of the labour movement began to talk of industrial action and a General Strike as the only way to stop the Tory attacks.

The Wales TUC decided that the only way to stop the Tory offensive against steel jobs — an offensive which also poses the threat of the closure of the entire South Wales coalfield, and the cutting of thousands of livelihoods dependent on the steel and coal industries — was general strike action. The same conviction that general action is necessary to stop the Tories led, at a meeting of the South Yorkshire Association of Trades Councils and the South Yorkshire Labour Parties, to a call for a general strike in their area for one day on February 18th (1980).

Moving according to the same line of thought, the Scottish TUC scheduled a half-day strike for February 13th, though it then put it off.

On November 28th 1979 60,000 struck work to demonstrate against the cuts, responding to the TUC and Labour Party call. On September 13, many workers joined a borough-wide strike and day of action against the cuts in Hackney, East London. They too saw the need for all-round class action to counter the all-round Tory offensive.

A general strike could pull together the partial responses so far — none of them quite coming to grips with the scale of the Tory offensive — into a mighty power. In place of the havering and dithering which has characterised labour movement resistance to the Tories so far, we would have full mobilisation of our strength against their full mobilisation of their strength.

The growing murmur for a general strike moves indicates that, within six months of the return of a Tory government to power, the labour movement has had to begin to rediscover the direct industrial action reflexes it learned to use as the only reliable political weapon to hand in 1969-74.

It is still only beginning, and there have been some setbacks. But the hard facts of a Tory assault in the midst of economic crisis must inevitably drive the labour movement to rediscover the powerful experience of using industrial action directly for political ends which it built up in the struggle against *In Place of Strife* and then in the battles against Heath's Tories.

Now, even more than in the period after June 1970, we face a vicious and reactionary Tory government with the knuckledusters on for the

WHAT REVOLUTIONARY SOCIALISTS ADVOCATED AGAINST THATCHER

working class. Motivated by middle-class spite and blind bourgeois economics, and driven on by the desperate state of the British economy, they are making the working class pay for British capitalism's crisis and for the Tories' quack solutions.

At the same time, their anti-union laws strike a first blow aimed to weaken the ability of the labour movement to resist and defend itself.

They build on the policies of the Wilson/Callaghan governments and add their own vicious twists. Encouraged by an electoral victory which was handed to them by the right wing policies of Callaghan's government, they have moved to make the third attempt in a decade to shackle the trade union movement.

Now — exactly as in 1970 and after — we face a militant class-struggle Tory government, firmly entrenched behind a large and stable Parliamentary majority and backed by all the military and police power of the British state. They are determined to make war on the standards, conditions, and organisations of the working class. In their attack on our class they will use to the full their legal right to make the laws and control the finances of the state.

Either the labour movement will allow this Tory government with its programme of blatant ruling-class legislation to rule and administer society in the interests of the class they represent — even to the extent of the movement obeying anti-trade-union laws in the hope that, maybe, five years from now. perhaps a Labour government will be voted in which may undo some of the Tory damage.

Or the movement will fight back here and now recognising no Tory or ruling class right to meddle with the trade unions, to cut into the standards which the working class has won in decades of activity, or to destroy whole working class communities through closure policies. It will refuse to keep within the normal channels of official politics. It will resist the Tories' attacks by every means necessary.

For a start, that means the labour movement must break off collaboration with the government and use the strength and power which we have now and can choose to unleash, irrespective of who has the majority in Parliament. That means using industrial action to stop the Tories in their tracks. Just like we did last time round.

It is because these are the only alternatives here and now and for the foreseeable future that sections of the labour movement have begun to raise demands for an industrial offensive and talk of a general strike is again heard.

To be sure, talk of the need for "the big industrial battalions" to go into action against the Tories can be used as a cop-out by people who want to avoid a fight here and now, in their own areas.

Some left councillors excused their own unwillingness to refuse to carry out cuts last summer with such talk. Joe Gormley called for a general strike in 1973 as a basis for arguing against the miners alone going into action.

It is necessary to fight now and on every front, at the same time as we argue for general industrial action and prepare for it.

The labour movement needs to develop, and organise round, an overall strategy to stop the Tories. For Thatcher can be stopped, just as Heath was stopped.

In the first place, we need to spell out and win support in the labour movement for this immediate objective — to stop the Tories, to force them to retreat, to defeat their attacks, to stop their closure policies decimating working class communities, to make them abandon their cuts policies, to break their will, to thwart their plans, and to drive them from office as soon as possible.

The outrageous anti-working class politics of this Government demand from the entire political and industrial labour movement — from every section of it which claims to represent the working class interest, all the way through to the Parliamentary Labour Party and the Shadow Cabinet — a refusal to collaborate with the Tory government and its agents, backed up by offensive actions to kick out the Government.

The movement must demand that its leaders really fight the Tories, and really fight for Labour Party policies. And we must be prepared to break with those who refuse to fight, and get rid of them.

Such a policy, accompanied by a Labour and trade union campaign to explain the issues and to mobilise the working class, could have a tremendous effect.

Despite some setbacks, industrial action, or talk of industrial action, against cuts and closures, is already beginning to be a normal response. We need to generalise such responses, to link up the different battalions in conflict with the Tory government. In short, we need to' concentrate the power of the labour movement.

The Wales TUC is absolutely right. A general strike could at the very least force the Tories to change course on trade union laws, on closures, on cuts, or on all of these policies.

In July 1972 the Government quickly changed its mind and released the five dockers jailed under the Industrial Relations Act, in response to a spontaneous strike wave of a few hundred thousand workers and the mere threat by the TUC to stage a one-day general strike.

In theory, if its parliamentary majority held, as it probably would, the Tory government might remain in office after such a defeat. In fact, though, defeat would put the skids under the government and probably drive it from office.

And the level of self-mobilisation needed to allow the working class to defeat this entrenched government would open, up tremendous possibilities beyond the limited objectives of defeating Tory policies or even of defeating the Tory government itself.

A general strike is more serious than a sectional strike. It challenges directly and openly the bosses' right to make and enforce the law. Implicitly it poses the question of who is master in the country, and explicitly it challenges the automatic right of the ruling class to control the general affairs of society.

If the Tories are in power after such a defeat, they would quickly counterattack. So indeed would a right wing Labour government based on Parliament and committed to the capitalist system, should such a government be installed as the result of the working class offensive. (The 1974-9 Labour government continued the build-up of police power started under Heath).

But that would be the round after this one. The job now is to win this round. The experience before 1974 showed us how we can win it. After we win, we will be stronger to face any counterattacks.

Concretely, what can we do?

• Support strike action and occupations against the cuts, closures, etc.

• Demand that it be generalised, and that the TUC prepare a general strike. Where other strike action is planned, bring it forward to link up with the general action.

• Argue within the unions and the Labour Party for a full scale offensive to stop the Tories, using the strength we have here and now, refusing collaboration.

Demand that the Parliamentary Labour leaders start a campaign of Parliamentary obstruction. Demand they pledge themselves to complete repeal of the Tory anti-union laws and to restoration of all Tory cuts when they return to office.

Demand the TUC leaders break off their cosy chats with the Tories in the National Economic Development Council and dozens of other governmental and industrial "participation" bodies. No talks on the anti-union Bill: start a fightback! Demand the TUC withdraws its Guidelines on picketing. Demand that Labour councils defy the Tory cuts.

We must call for the leaders of the trade union movement and the National Executive of the Labour Party to launch such a campaign to stop the Tories, including preparation for a general strike. We must be prepared to fight to remove Parliamentarians, councillors, and trade union leaders who collaborate and cooperate with the Tories.

• We ourselves — the militants, the socialists — must prepare on a local level, now. A general strike will be won through the network of workers' committees and organisations, most of which exist already as part of the routine self-defence and self-betterment of the working class: stewards' committees, combine committees, etc. We must transfuse into these bodies the urgency of preparing for a head-on clash with the Tories, and equip them with the necessary democratic structure and flexibility to mobilise millions of workers for that clash.

• We must build and renew links between the Labour Parties and the trade union organisation in the workplaces. We must build workplace Labour Party branches.

* We must fight to rearm the labour movement politically with socialist policies, with the sort of working-class demands fought for by Socialist Organiser and the Socialist Campaign for a Labour Victory.

The labour movement must in fact represent a real alternative to the Tories, so that there can be no repeat of the tragic and dismal experience of 1974 and after — when a Labour government, returned as a result of a huge wave of working class militancy, carried through essentially Tory policies and demobilised and disheartened its supporters.

Socialist Organiser no. 15, January 1980

We need a workers' government!

In the wake of the 1980 Labour Party conference, which saw an unprecedented rank-and-file surge to democratise the party, Socialist Organiser *(forerunner of AWL) called for a fight for a workers' government.*

Tony Benn drew an enormous amount of fire from the press with his speech on behalf of the [Labour Party] National Executive Committee at the opening of the Blackpool Labour Party conference. To read the hacks, and listen to the baying of the Press Lords, you'd be forgiven for thinking that Benn had delivered a paraphrase of the Communist Manifesto of Marx and Engels, or of its latter-day supplement, the 1938 Programme of Leon Trotsky. You'd be wrong. Dead wrong.

Benn proposed three emergency measures to be enacted immediately the next Labour government takes office.

• The abolition of the House of Lords.

• A wide-ranging Industry Bill, to be put on the statute books "within a matter of days". This would give the next Labour government power (by decree) to extend public ownership, control capital movements, and "provide for" "industrial democracy".

• Within a matter of weeks, a Bill would be enacted to return to the House of Commons the powers which it has surrendered to the Common Market in the last seven years.

All this would be done constitutionally and according to the present rules. There would be no ringing Roundhead declaration of the democratic right of the House of Commons, as an elected Parliament, simply to dismiss the Lords. 1000 new Lords would be created to get the 'consent' of the House of Lords.

The package amounts to no more than a limited strengthening of the House of Commons. It is limited indeed, because it would leave the monarchy in being, together with its quite substantial reserve powers. (For example, what if the monarch refused to create 1000 peers?). In any major social conflicts, the formal powers of the monarchy would be a natural rallying point for the reactionaries. The package also contains nothing about even curbing the power of the civil service or of the armed forces.

How radically does Benn conceive of the Industry Act being used? If a firm is unable to provide jobs when all around us the lives of millions of working class families and whole working class communities are being devastated, it would seem to be a pretty clear indication that private ownership in that industry should not continue. Yet at the Labour conference Tony Benn successfully opposed a proposal that any firms threatening redundancies should be nationalised under workers' control. The recent National Executive Committee rolling manifesto omitted Labour's policy for nationalising 25 big monopolies.

Tony Benn's programme is ridiculously inadequate as a socialist or working class response to the situation we face.

British society is rotting and decaying all around us, and the Tory government is now deliberately acting as a demolition squad. It is not only that the Tories lack feeling for the British people, though they are sustained in their work by a brutal upper-class callousness towards the workers. More fundamentally, the desperate decline of Britain, fundamentally the decline of British industry's competitiveness and profitability, makes desperate measures necessary — and for the Tories desperate measures are measures that make the workers pay.

The repeated failures of different government strategies, Labour and Tory, prepared the way for demolition-squad Toryism. Just as mortally-ill people sometimes resort to the most outlandish quackery, the main party of British capitalism opts for the murderous quackery of monetarism because they believe that all the other options have closed for them.

Only one thing can fundamentally change the situation for British capitalism in the period ahead — the driving down of the working class share in the wealth we produce to a dramatic degree and at least a serious weakening of the trade unions. For example, it is because they hope that it will help them in these aims, that the Tories are so ready to tolerate and increase unemployment and the massive destruction of the social fabric that accompanies it.

Labour in office prepared the way for Thatcher. Not just in the obvious sense that Healey and Callaghan introduced their own savage cuts in 1976 and 77, but by its thoroughgoing failure to regenerate industry and British society.

Put into office in the wave of industrial direct action that scuttled Heath, the government behaved as a straight-line capitalist government. It abused the confidence of the workers. Basing itself on the trade union bureaucracy (until 1978) at one side and the state machine on the other, it ruled in defiance of Labour Party conference decisions. It got wage "restraint" and actually cut real wages for two years running.

But what the ruling class learned from that experience was the insufficiency of even a relatively successful (in their terms) Labour government. They needed to make the sort of attacks Labour could not make without shattering its base. Thus Thatcherism.

Against Thatcherism, the Labour Left now has a near consensus in favour of trying another policy for running capitalism — it will have a different driver, a state wheel added here, and a few control screws tightened or added there. But it will remain capitalist.

Import controls, state intervention perhaps to the level reached in wartime Britain, and the collaboration of the working class (read restraint; read incomes policy, perhaps cosmeticised by some regulations on profit distribution) are supposed to ensure the regeneration of British industry and society.

This is nothing but edition three of the sort of delusion that dominated the 1964-70 and 1974-9 Labour governments. In so far as they administered capitalism at all successfully, it was by attacking the working class; and they failed miserably to arrest the decline of British industry and society.

The time for patching is long past — and in any case it is in the working class interest not to patch but to transform and bring about fundamental change towards democratic working class socialism — that irreversible change in the balance of wealth and power that the 1974 manifesto tantalisingly talked about and Labour in power forgot all about.

We must replace the fundamental mechanism of capitalism — profit — with a new one: the needs of the working people, fulfilled in a society organised, owned collectively, and run democratically by the working class. This demands that we plan our lives by planning and organising the economy on which we must build our lives, and this in turn demands the social ownership of the land and major industries. We need a radical working class alternative to capitalism.

Whether the next Labour government — in 1984, or earlier if we do as we have the industrial strength to do and kick out Thatcher — will be a more or less radical new instalment of the sort of Labour governments we have had this century, or not, will be determined by two things:

• By whether a real attack is made on the wealth and entrenched power of the ruling class; and,

• by whether or not it rests at least in part on the organisations of the working class instead of on those of the state bureaucracy, the military, and Parliament — that is, whether in response to the direct demands of the working class it can do what we want, or endorse what we do (taking over factories, for example) without being a captive of the state machine.

The working class itself would serve and protect its own interests by organising itself outside the rhythms, norms, and constraints of Parliamentary politics, expanding its factory shop stewards' committees, combine committees, Trades Councils, etc., and creating new action committees, to be an industrial power that could as necessary dispense with the Parliamentarians.

The Brighton/Blackpool decisions to control MPs and to give the majority of votes on who shall be prime minister if Labour has a majority in Parliament to the CLPs and trade unions (if we are not cheated) could open the way to a new kind of "Labour" government — a workers' government — instead of a government of the trade union party which merely administers capitalism according to capitalism's own laws.

Revolutionary Marxists believe that there must be a socialist revolution — a clean sweep of the capitalists and the establishment of the state power of the working class, in workers' democracy. The big majority of the labour movement don't yet share our views. But we have a common need and determination to oppose and fight the Tory government and to oppose any moves, even by the Labour Party in government, to load the cost of capitalist decay and crisis onto the shoulders of the working class.

If we cannot agree on a root-and-branch transformation (or on precisely how to go about getting it), we can at least agree on a whole range of measures to protect ourselves and to cut down and control the capitalists.

To get the most out of the breakthrough for democracy at Brighton and Blackpool, we must fight to ensure that the next Labour government does act radically in our interests and does base itself on the movement, not on the bosses' state bureaucracy. And at the same time we must prepare and organise ourselves to be able to protect our own interests however it acts.

We must fight to commit the Party to radical socialist policies, and use reselection to make sure MPs are held to those policies. But if the Labour Party really were to strike at the power and wealth of the bosses, they would strike back, using their army and state forces to repress the movement if necessary — or simply to cow the Labour government.

Whoever wants to break out of the limits defined by the interests of the capitalists must be prepared to disarm the ruling class and destroy its state. Only the working class can do that, organised in squads like those which the flying pickets organise, which can arm themselves when necessary.

Any Parliament-based government that attempted really radical change would put its head on the block, and while the present armed forces exist the axe is in the hands of the bourgeoisie.

Alarmist? An intrusion of insurrectionary politics that are out of place in Britain? Unfortunately, no. In the last decade the Army has become highly politicised through its work in Northern Ireland. Early this year the pacifist Pat Arrowsmith debated with Field Marshal Carver, chief of the British Army during the struggles that got Heath out in 1974.

"Fairly senior officers", said Carver, "were ill-advised enough to make suggestions that perhaps, if things got terribly bad, the army would have to do something about it..." So it is either resign yourself to Thatcherism (or a new edition of Healey- Callaghan, or worse) — or fight on all fronts.

The power of the ruling class is not entirely, nor even essentially, in Parliament. That is the terrain to which they now go out from their redoubts in industry, the civil service and the armed forces, to meet and to parley with the labour movement, and to put on a show for the people.

But if the labour movement insists on new rules for the parleying game, they have a reserve language to resort to force. So have we.

But the bosses' greatest real strength is that they have convinced the majority of the people that force is no part — not even a reserve part — of British politics. That was not the view of the officers in 1974. The top brass told them then to shut up. But they won't always: some of the coup-talkers in 1974 are themselves now the top brass. In any case we should not rely on their restraint.

Thus we see that Labour's decisions on Party democracy and the new attitude to Parliament open the possibility of a new type of "Labour" government. But only the possibility.

With the present political positions of the Party and the leaders of its left, you would get a Labour government which would fundamentally be more of the same with radical trimmings. It would not serve the working class, and in present conditions it would not be able to adequately serve the ruling class. It would not even placate them. Neither the ruling class nor the working class can afford to muddle along indefinitely — or for much longer.

If Thatcherism fails to regenerate Britain — and it will fail, because of its own vicious absurdities and because the working class must make it fail — that will only increase the desperation of the ruling class. There is no room left for reformist tinkering.

In the last decade and a half, the working class has defeated successive attempts by Wilson and Heath to solve British capitalism's crisis and decay at our expense. We even drove Heath from office. The tragedy is that, while strong enough industrially to stop their solutions, we have not been politically able to develop a thoroughgoing working-class socialist solution.

The result is the sort of stalemate that has often in history been the prelude to attempts at ruling-class "solutions" through military coups or fascism. One cannot foresee or predict how long the present stalemate will continue. It is certain only that — if all past experience has any bearing on what will happen in Britain — it cannot continue indefinitely. A solution to the decay and crisis must be found, and it will either be theirs, or ours — that is, working-class reconstruction of society on a socialist basis.

The drive to clinch the decisions on Labour democracy is the centre of the struggle now. Unless the Labour Party is thoroughly democratised, talking about it now as a vehicle for struggle and change is as absurd as calling for the Labour Party to come "to power with socialist policies" was in the 60s and 70s. The Blackpool decisions must be consolidated, extended, and made to work. And no Labour democracy can be secure unless the trade unions are democratised. The rank and file militants in the unions must be organised.

But if we do not simultaneously organise a drive for the minimally necessary socialist policies, then the consequences of democratisation may well be very unlike what the left expects.

As Tony Benn said at Blackpool, a Labour Government will be tested by the banks, the IMF, etc., from the first hours. If it does not go on the offensive in the working class interest, against the capitalists and their system, then it will have to go on the offensive against the left in the labour movement.

Accountability can mean — as it does in European social-democratic parties — tight central control to keep the hands of the leaders free. If there had been accountability in 1975 when Jack Jones and the trade union bureaucracy collaborated with the government to set up the £6 pay limit, then there would have had to be a purge of the left (such as newspapers like the *Sunday Express* and *Observer* did try to launch).

With accountability, the leaders would not have the option of placidly ignoring the Party, as after 1975. The right and centre, even backed by the big unions, would have difficulty carrying through such a purge. But the point to focus on now is that it is a serious possibility unless we step up the drive to arm the movement — or at least big sections of its rank and file — with socialist politics.

And not at the "next stage". If the labour movement is to be ready to offer a real socialist alternative at the "next stage", its foundations must be laid and built upon now, and urgently. That is what the Socialist Organiser groups exist to do, and what we are trying to do.

Socialist Organiser no.28, 25 October 1980

Baksheesh:
Trotsky's Diary in Exile (1935)

A review by Michael Foot

"Only a participant can be a profound spectator," wrote Leon Trotsky.

He was contrasting the novels of Jules Romains with those of Emile Zola. Romains himself had referred to his distance from the scenes he described, and Trotsky points out that this distance was not only optical but also moral. Zola, the participant, was "deeper, warmer, and more human" and, therefore, the greater writer.

Trotsky himself, of course, is the foremost example of his own aphorism. He is, probably in all history, the greatest man of action who was also a very great literary genius.

Everything he wrote bears the individual stamp of the man; it has a pulse and urgency which is absent from the writings of those political writers, even the most perceptive, who were only spectators.

This applies to the latest Trotsky "discovery," the fragments of a diary he wrote during his exile in France and Norway in 1935, even though he obviously found the diary form awkward and distasteful.

By comparison with his finest writings, Trotsky's *Diary in Exile* is slight and rambling. But it still wins a considerable place in socialist literature.

At first, its chief interest is contained in the numerous side-glancing insights into casual occurrences. For example:

Trotsky and his wife go to Lourdes:

"What crudeness, insolence, nastiness! A shop for miracles, a business office for trafficking in Grace. The Grotto itself makes a miserable impression. That, of course, is a psychological calculation of the clerics; not to frighten the little people away by the grandeur of their commercial enterprise; little people are afraid of shop windows that are too resplendent. At the same time they are the most faithful and profitable customers. But best of all is the papal blessing broadcast to Lourdes by — radio. The paltry miracles of the Gospels side by side with the radio-telephone! And what could be more absurd and disgusting than the union of proud technology with the sorcery of the Roman chief druid. Indeed the thinking of mankind is bogged down in its own excrement."

Or his recalled conversation with Kamenev about Stalin:

"'Do you think that Stalin is now considering how to reply to your arguments?' This was approximately what Kamenev said, in reference to my criticism of the Stalin-Bukharin-Molotov policies in China, England, etc. 'You are mistaken. He is thinking of how to destroy you.'"

Or his foresight about the fall of France:

"March 21. It's spring, the sun is hot, the violets have been in bloom for about ten days, the peasants are puttering around in the vineyards. Last night we listened to Die Walkür from Bourdeaux until midnight. Military service extended to two years. Rearmament of Germany. Preparations for a new 'final' war. The peasants peacefully prune their vines and fertilize the furrows between them. Everything is in order.

"The Socialists and the Communists write articles against the two-year term, and for the sake of greater impressiveness trot out their largest type. Deep in their hearts the 'leaders' hope things will work out somehow. Here also everything is in order.

"And yet this order has hopelessly undermined itself. It will collapse with a stench ..."

Or his comments on Marx and Engels:

"When you have had enough of the prose of the Blums, the Cachins, and the Thorezes, when you have swallowed your fill of the microbes of pettiness and insolence, obsequiousness and ignorance, there is no better way of clearing your lungs than by reading the correspondence of Marx and Engels, both to each other and to other people. In their epigrammatic allusions and characterizations, sometimes paradoxical, but always well thought out and to the point, there is so much instruction, so much mental freshness and mountain air! They always lived on the heights."

Such quotations could be endlessly multiplied. But there is also a recurring theme running through the diary which makes it a document of excruciating poignancy.

In his autobiography Trotsky wrote one of the most moving accounts of a man's childhood which has ever been written. Here, in the diary, he has painted an incomparable picture of his wife, Natasha.

The hunt of Trotsky's children and his friends by Stalin is surely one of the most appalling stories of sustained barbaric revenge of which history has any record. The full brunt of the horror fell on the heart of the dignified and dauntless Natasha.

Quotation would mar this immortal tribute of a man to his wife. Read it for yourself.

Originally published in *Tribune*, 17 June 1959.

Michael Foot: the man who embraced defeat to avoid defeat

Sean Matgamna

It was a tragedy for the British working class and its labour movement that Michael Foot, who has died at the age of 96, was its political leader when it faced its life-and-death confrontation with Thatcherism at the beginning of the 1980s.

By that stage in his long journalistic career — 70 years ago he was already editor of the *London Evening Standard* — and long political life, Foot was a burnt-out, time-serving ex-radical, deeply mired in political horse trading with the Liberals and Ulster Unionists to keep the Callaghan Government (1974-79) in power.

Compared to the spineless, colourless, principle-free mainstream politicians of today, Foot was a "man of principle", as the obituarists insist. In contrast to today's narrow-minded, small-souled gangs of political technicians scrambling for office, Michael Foot was a man of broad mind and generous sympathies. And in his own way he was loyal to the working class and the labour movement.

But as a working-class leader Michael Foot was a disaster.

When he became Labour leader Foot told a mass rally in Liverpool that the Labour Party would raise a storm of indignation that would drive the Tories from office. In fact he did the very opposite.

Two incidents from that time epitomised what Foot, the political leader of the labour movement from 1980, was by then.

Peter Tatchell, the official Labour candidate in a by-election in the London district of Bermondsey, was targeted in the press as a man who believed in political direct action (and in some of the press and on the ground in Bermondsey he was subjected to a campaign of savage gay-baiting). In the House of Commons, Tatchell's party leader, Foot, denounced and repudiated him. Tatchell went on to lose the by-election in what had been a safe Labour seat.

In the second typical incident, at the beginning of 1982, Labour Party leader Foot contributed a two-part article to the *Observer*, in which he told the British workers that direct action to resist a properly-elected government, Thatcher's government, was democratically impermissible. This was a government that legislated to outlaw effective trade unionism — sympathetic strike action — and was intent on smashing up the labour movement.

Foot told the working class movement not to use the only weapon it had between general elections, industrial direct action, and not to resist a militantly anti-working-class bourgeois government which was using state power in almost a Jacobin fashion to remodel society and break the back of the labour movement!

The serious class warrior, Margaret Thatcher, would in the course of the struggle with the working class deploy as much violence as she found necessary to beat down working-class resistance

During the miners' strike the Tory Government would send semi-militarised police to occupy rebellious mining villages and police cavalry to defeat picketing miners in pitched battles such as the Battle of Orgreave, in mid-1984.

But Labour leader Foot told the labour movement that to defeat Thatcher by direct action, as we had defeated Thatcher's predecessor Edward Heath, would be a crime against democracy, and Foot's hand-picked successor as Labour leader, no-guts Neil Kinnock, played the Tory game by adding his voice to the denunciations of the miners, who were themselves victims of state violence, for their "violence".

Foot was finally driven off the central political stage after the 1983 General Election amidst a barrage of press jeering and mockery because he had appeared in public in what looked like a donkey jacket. It was brutally unjust, as was so much of the press commentary on the labour movement and on the left.

Foot had been a central leader of the early campaign for nuclear disarmament. Here too, he led the retreat in deference to an established order. That time, the Labour Party establishment.

When in 1960 the left won the bulk of the unions at the Labour Party Conference to support British nuclear disarmament, the Parliamentary Labour Party, led by party leader Hugh Gaitskell, refused to accept the Conference decision and threatened to split the Party. Foot retreated with the cry: "never underestimate the desire of the Labour Party for unity", and the result was that the right wing reversed the 1960 decision at the 1961 Conference.

Foot had seen better times. He was one of Nye Bevan's chief lieutenants in the great days of the leftwing Labour upsurge in the 1950s. He was editor of the then-Bevanite journal *Tribune*. He worked with the

Trotskyists and led a vigorous campaign inside the Labour Party against the banning of their paper *Socialist Outlook* in 1954.

He stood up to the Stalinist avalanche of lies against Trotsky and the other Bolsheviks, long before it became fashionable to do that, in the mid-1950s, after Stalin's successor Khrushchev had denounced him as a crazed mass murderer.

Foot, like most of the Labour left then, had been a sympathiser with Stalinism in the late 1930s and early 1940s. And he was a victim of Stalinism.

Disillusioned, he came to identify Stalinism with the Russian Revolution, and "revolution" per se with Stalinism. The Russian Revolution, and the violence of the revolutionary workers against the old ruling classes was the "original sin" that led to Stalinism. Parliamentarianism and legality was the only safe course for socialists to pursue.

It was a paralysing philosophy for a working-class leader faced with the onslaught of Thatcher. Foot and other Labour people then, union leader Jack Jones for instance, feared a military coup in Britain, like that of Chile in September 1973, if they went all-out to resist Thatcher. Later Jack Jones would admit and publicly discuss this. In fear of that, they accepted crushing defeat without a fight — accepting defeat to avoid defeat! We are still suffering the consequences of that defeat without a fight.

Solidarity, 5 March 2010